A TESOL Professional Anthology:

Culture

Edited by
Carol Cargill

National Textbook Company
a division of *NTC Publishing Group* • Lincolnwood, Illinois USA

OTHER BOOKS IN THIS SERIES:

A TESOL Professional Anthology: Grammar and Composition
A TESOL Professional Anthology: Listening, Speaking, and Reading

1992 Printing

Published by National Textbook Company, a division of NTC Publishing Group,
© 1987 by NTC Publishing Group, 4255 West Touhy Avenue,
Lincolnwood (Chicago), Illinois 60646-1975 USA.
Manufactured in the United States of America.
Library of Congress Catalog Card Number: 86-60914

2 3 4 5 6 7 8 9 0 VP 9 8 7 6 5 4 3 2

Preface

THIS BOOK is one of a three-volume series of professional references for teachers, program directors, and teacher-trainers. Although many books are already available in the field of teaching English to speakers of other languages (variously referred to as ESOL, ESL, or EFL), no one work can provide information on every aspect of teaching the language.

Each volume in this series focuses on one or more specific components of the language learning process. This book looks at the cultural aspects of language learning. Another volume focuses on listening, speaking, and reading development, while the third book in the series looks at the development of grammar and composition skills. Each book is a collection of papers written by outstanding professionals in the field of English language education. Collectively, the authors have amassed approximately two centuries worth of teaching experience. Their messages are an invaluable contribution to the pool of knowledge available to help new and inexperienced teachers become better at their profession.

The material contained within these pages also provides practical information for in-service teachers who want to update their understanding of the dynamics of English in a second-language setting.

All of the authors are or have been classroom teachers. Many of them are also methodologists who are involved in teacher-training programs and have seen the value of sharing their experience and ideas with colleagues who are preparing to enter the field. The goal of this series is to provide a more widespread forum for the sharing of professional knowledge and experience in the field of teaching English to speakers of other languages.

CONTRIBUTORS TO THIS VOLUME

CAROL CARGILL is Director of the Graduate Program in Applied Linguistics (TESL) and Director of the International Language Institute at the University of South Florida in Tampa.

LINDA EVANS is an ESL Instructor for the International Language Institute at the University of South Florida in Tampa.

KATHERINE RICHMOND is a doctoral candidate in Reading Education in the College of Education at the University of South Florida in Tampa.

ROGER W. COLE is a Professor of Linguistics for the International Language Institute at the University of South Florida in Tampa.

ANGELA LUPO-ANDERSON is Director/Program Review for the State University System of Florida.

DAN McCAULEY is an Instructor for the United States Army Dependent Schools in Guam.

ERNEST FRECHETTE is a Professor of Education with the Multi-lingual Educational Center at Florida State University in Tallahassee.

CHARLES M. BAILEY is an ESL Instructor for the International Language Institute at the University of South Florida in Tampa.

LUZ PAREDES LONO is Curriculum Coordinator for the International Language Institute at the University of South Florida in Tampa.

PAULA W. SUNDERMAN is an Associate Professor of English at Mississippi State University in Mississippi State.

DAVID W. GURNEY is an Associate Professor of Foreign Languages at the University of Central Florida in Orlando.

Contents

Introduction

CAROL CARGILL

T HE SUBJECT OF THIS volume is culture in the English-language program. Some of the authors discuss the positive aspects of culture
as part of the ESL curriculum. Others point out the negative aspects of
culture, such as when it cloaks bias in tests. Some approach culture
from the point of view of the multicultural classroom. Culture is an
important aspect of any program for limited English speakers, whether they be refugees or international students, migrants or students of
English as a foreign language in a distant land.

Cultural bias in testing has been a focal point of many researchers
and teachers. In the first article, Carol Cargill points out a number of
pitfalls to the classroom teacher who may be unaware of them. She
discusses particular types of tests which may be biased against a
certain group of students. Linda S. Evans discusses elementary school
ESL programs that include students from several different ethnic
backgrounds. She points out the difficulties LEP students face as they
encounter various aspects of American culture. Further, she poses the
question of whose culture should be taught in a variety of settings.

Katherine Richmond discusses expectations that ESL teachers com-
monly have—expectations which may or may not be accurate. When
a teacher's expectations do not match the cultural characteristics of a
student or a group of students, misconceptions can occur. Richmond
urges teachers to recognize culture-related problems involving their

own feelings toward their students as well as those involving the students' attitudes toward the culture represented by the teacher. She identifies some coping skills which will assist ESL teachers in dealing with culture-based problems, along with some practical suggestions drawn from her involvement with programs for Choctaw Indians in Mississippi.

How does a difference in culture affect pre-literates? This topic is explored by Roger W. Cole in his chapter. Cole identifies problems posed by traditional programs that are geared to students who are literate in their native languages. He points out the inadequacy of such programs for pre-literates and provides practical recommendations for teaching the English language as a tool not just for communication but also for learning a vocation or job skill.

Angela Lupo-Anderson discusses the misconceptions that surround bilingual education. She identifies approaches to bicultural programs as part of bilingual education and highlights the importance of disciplines such as music and art which lend themselves to sharing cross-culturally. Other aspects of the bicultural or multicultural class are discussed in the chapter by Dan McCauley. He asks what degree of responsibility for preserving students' native cultures should be assumed by a school's administration or policy. He also questions the merit of cultural relativism and labels it possible moral relativism. McCauley identifies areas of political dispute regarding bilingual education as well as educational strategies based on a linguistic perspective.

Ernest Frechette concurs that teachers must know about the native cultures of their students, and he provides important information about the Saudi culture. He defines the role of religion as it influences Saudi behavior and describes social relations and taboos. Obligations regarding work and attitudes toward certain types of work are also discussed. Frechette includes a helpful list of comparisons and contrasts between the Saudi and American cultures.

Charles M. Bailey describes a case study conducted in New Bedford, Massachusetts. The cultural appropriateness of one approach to teaching English to a group of Portuguese immigrants is the subject of his study. He praises the notional-functional approach as being suitable for any age or level of instruction. The fact that this approach contains a cultural component is pointed out in the examples he gives. Mere cultural immersion is criticized as not being sufficient to give the newcomer confidence in the new environment; Bailey says that explicit cultural input must be provided and can be provided through a notional-functional syllabus.

Developing reading skills for the limited English proficient student is the focus of the chapter by Luz Paredes Lono. She discusses the complexities of the reading skill, pointing out that comprehension relies not only on linguistic mastery but also on mastery of cultural content. If a student cannot relate to a cultural context in a reading passage, he or she will not be able to comprehend and react as expected, Lono says.

Paula W. Sunderman looks at culture as a necessary part of any ESL/EFL curriculum. Sunderman accuses education in general of failing to provide the cultural component necessary to international students in engineering and business, in particular. Knowledge of how culture relates to the various disciplines studied by foreign students in the U.S. is important, Sunderman says. While science may be considered "culture free," scientists working in a multicultural or bicultural environment need special skills to interact in such a setting. These skills must be taught in school, because the necessary training seldom takes place after a new employee begins working for a multinational corporation.

Openness toward other cultures is the topic of David W. Gurney's chapter. Gurney views education as a forum for accepting input from visitors to the U.S. He emphasizes that it is important for foreign students to take part in the sharing process when it comes to cultural aspects of their lives. He calls for cultural empathy in teacher training and includes a list of factors which should be understood by any ESL teacher. Gurney's remarks are particularly valuable for high school programs involving exchange students. In addition, they may have an important bearing on adult exchange programs and programs designed for immigrants or foreign students who will spend a number of years in the U.S.

Cultural Bias in Testing ESL

CAROL CARGILL

T HERE ARE POTENTIAL DANGERS in culture coding tests. While language instruction should not be devoid of cultural content, cultural bias and culture coding may yield unreliable test results. There are various ways in which a test may be culturally biased. A culture-coded test is one which requires students to know something outside the intended forms being tested. Its validity is questionable because some extra-linguistic information is required of the students in order to answer correctly.

An example of the dangers of such material could be a placement test in which oral production is tested by means of picture cues. The picture cue calling for the correct grammatical response is preceded by a different picture cue with a similar scene. For example, the students taking this test first see a picture of a boy smiling. The students are told, "The boy is happy." The students are then shown another picture cue with a girl smiling. If they are expected to answer "The girl is happy," the test is heavily culture coded; it would certainly be of doubtful reliability in assessing the students' ability to translate that picture cue into the idea that the person in the picture is happy. We know in American culture that a smiling face usually means that a person is happy. However, experience in Vietnamese integration programs shows that a smiling Vietnamese boy may not be happy; he may be embarrassed, confused, or even angry.

1

Fortunately, this particular test was developed by Marie DeShields Jawardi (Arlington County Schools, Virginia), an experienced teacher whose aim was *not* to elicit only the response "The boy is happy," which would have been culturally unfair. In fact, this test was structurally controlled. The desired response was merely a form of the verb *to be* in the present tense. Acceptable responses would include

1. The boy is happy.
2. The boy is smiling.
3. He is happy.
4. He is smiling.

5. The boy's happy.
6. The boy's smiling.
7. He's happy.
8. He's smiling.

The test makers avoided culture coding by allowing even such answers as "He's tired." Such an answer demonstrates that, although the student failed to interpret the smile as a sign of happiness, he knows and can handle the third person singular present tense form of the verb *to be*.

What are the cultural pitfalls that should be avoided in language teaching and testing? In her presentation at the International Seminar on Language Testing (1973), E. Condon stated that culture teaching should include facts on civilization such as history, geography, and the arts. Culture, however, can be found not only in historical reading selections but also in what Condon calls explicit and implicit aspects of civilization. Explicit forms of culture include class distinctions, family relationships, housing practices, and eating habits. Implicit cultural information comes from culturally conditioned factors such as unspoken attitudes and beliefs, Condon says.

Such information may be without value in test making if the item is true in some regions or local communities but not widespread enough to be included in a test. Of course, references to local customs are encouraged in local teacher-made tests. However, cultural bias on the part of the teacher in the testing situation should be avoided. Today, in our highly mobile society, we are encouraged to situationalize teaching and testing experiences according to the realities our students will face. That is, our cultural input must be controlled for its relevance.

It must also be controlled for its accuracy in general. For example, the Comprehensive English Language Test (1970) included only 11 neutral items out of 35. The others showed American society characterized by rejection, anger, fear, and violence. While all these do appear in American life, the inclusion of so many cannot but influence the student's picture of the U.S. in a negative way, and stimulate *reflection* on these topics or reaction against them.

Many teachers draw their test material from textbooks, in order to control valid vocabulary for test items. However, textbooks may contain errors in reference to cultural background. While these items may have been correct at the time of the book's publication, they may no longer be accurate. For example, a statement that the Empire State Building is the tallest building in the world would have to be changed if accuracy in cultural content is desired. On the other hand, if the focus is on the superlative form "tallest," we might say that the misinformation serves as a distractor, but we will nevertheless receive the correct grammatical form.

Sometimes culture coding serves as more than a distractor; it serves as the main attraction. For example, in a well-known text in use today, there is an example which requires the students to know cultural background in order to answer with the correct structural feature. The grammatical point in focus is the comparative form. The sentence reads: "Davis has an interest in medieval art. He has been to both the Cloisters and the Museum of Modern Art. Naturally, the Cloisters are (more interesting)." This item requires the student to know that the Cloisters is a museum, and that it contains medieval art. A similar item requires the students to know about Yankee Stadium, the Polo Grounds, and Ebbetts Field.

Ideally, of course, informed and experienced test writers would have done an item analysis after this test was written and would have concluded that the index of difficulty was too high. Thus, the item would have been stricken.

Accuracy may be lost not only by using dated textbooks but also by using dated information which the teacher/testmaker possesses. For example, to refer once again to the issue of the tallest building, how many ESL teachers could accurately fill in the blank in the item "_____ is the tallest building in the world," given the choices (a) the Sears Tower and (b) the World Trade Centers. In this example there is no grammatical cue; therefore, the answer can only come from a cultural cue which the student has received outside the class (or at least outside the test).

Another possible area of teacher inaccuracies is geography. The world's borders are changing so fast in some areas that the teacher would be well advised to double-check information with the morning newspaper. Cultural input in classroom exercises and tests may be biased by the teacher's own ignorance.

Appropriateness of "hot" news items as a cultural setting for test items should be questioned. For example, some text writers have shown a lack of sensitivity to an event such as the assassination of President Kennedy. Is this information really appropriate as a back-drop for a test item? The painful event that took place in Ford's Theater over a century ago was probably avoided in other classes for a much longer period of mourning than would be expected in history classes. The use of current news as a backdrop for a grammatical exercise or test is open to criticism. It would not be condemned, of course, in a reading test for cultural background.

Culture-coded information on a test may also produce unreliable performance when test items describe settings which are typical of some American homes but unheard of in the native country of the international student. For example, in a test administered to Spanish-speaking students, a picture cue showing a boy volunteering to help his mother with the housework would not be acceptable. One might argue that the student studying in the U.S. should get used to such ideas, since they are acceptable here. However, the situation changes when this test item appears in a commercially produced test shipped to South America. Upon seeing this scene, a student would immediately be hit by culture shock. Is this healthy in a testing situation? What toll does it take from students' test scores?

Another example of cultural interference can occur when the test administration itself affects students' scores. For example, in most classrooms, students are allowed and even urged to ask questions during a test if they are too puzzled to go on. This is usually done without disturbing other students by raising the hand. Frequently a student will discover that last typographical error which we failed to find before test time. An American student would simply inquire, and the correction would be noted for the benefit of the whole class. (Fortunately, on standardized tests, such kinks have already been removed.) The freedom to ask questions during a test is absent in many cultures. Most foreign students would rather leave a section blank, and risk failing the test, before venturing to ask a simple question.

Culture shock may result from another aspect of test administration: the timing of the test itself. Many international students have not experienced timed tests until they take the Test of English as a Foreign Language (TOEFL). The reliability factor in a student's performance is certainly in question when he or she sits nervously, ever aware of the clock.

Culture coding also appears from the administrative point of view in the item types themselves, especially with multiple-choice and cloze items. As with the timed test, the student is at least temporarily confused, even given a battery of instructions explaining what a multiple-choice or cloze test requires.

Cloze testing has been used as an instrument to determine placement in language programs, language proficiency, reading readiness, and readability of material for international students. Alderson (1979) defines the term *cloze procedure* as being used in three different ways. The first and most general definition is "the systematic deletion of words from text," where "systematic" remains undefined. The second definition takes the word "systematic" and divides it into two types of systems: either a random (or pseudo-random) deletion of words, or a rational deletion. A third definition, which is increasingly common in the literature, is the deletion of every fifth word from the text (that is, not just pseudo-random, but a specific deletion frequency).

The scoring of a cloze test may vary. One method is to accept as correct only the exact word that was deleted from the text, ignoring misspellings. This is the most rigid method and, in my opinion, the one which tests memory span rather than comprehension. In most ESL testing situations using cloze, the exact word is *not* sought, but rather an appropriate synonym may be acceptable to show that the reader has comprehended the message. This seems to be the least biased procedure, and is neither too rigid nor too flexible. An overly flexible scoring procedure might allow any item of the same form class (the same grammatical category or part of speech) even if it does not logically fit in the slot. This method seems objectionable because it may reliably test the reader's perception of the morphological or syntactic rules of the language, but it fails to measure comprehension of the text.

The cloze test that admits as correct any word of a particular form class does not discriminate between students who have comprehended what they have read and those who simply recognize syntactic cues. The former selects a word which fits logically into the passage, while the latter gets the same credit for having a small amount of syntactic information and answering with an inappropriate noun in a space following the word *the*.

Cultural bias comes about when such a test is used to assess the language proficiency of a nonnative speaker. It also comes into play when such a test is used for placement purposes. For example, a student may exhibit a response which does not fit the format of the cloze procedure. The test solicits a single word response in each slot. Bias in test format may appear with groups such as Thai students. Their language does not mark word boundaries as we know them. Therefore, Thai students tend to make more errors on cloze tests than students from other language groups, because they fill in the blanks with multiple word entries (Oller 1972). In doing so, they cannot even get credit for the correct form class since the syntactic structures they use are so complex that they obscure any identification of form class.

We know from comparisons between cloze tests and other standardized tests designed for proficiency or placement that there is a low correlation between them and cloze when used with certain students. Which type of test is unreliable? My research, which examines the results of cloze tests based on level of proficiency and cultural ethno-linguistic background, suggests that cloze tests are often unreliable.

What can be done to avoid these problems? American students taking the SAT or ACT are also victims of nervousness the first time around. We routinely advise them to take the exams in their junior year in order to become familiar with timed, multiple-choice tests, and to allow extra time for re-taking the exam(s) if needed. Should we not advise our international students to allow extra time as well? Of course, many ESL students *do* take required standardized tests more than once. Moreover, tests should cover only what they are intended to test; otherwise, they lose validity and reliability. Tests which show the students' ability to perform and manipulate the format first and the content second should be avoided.

In summary, cultural content is necessary in language instruction. It is unavoidable as a backdrop for good language testing. It should at least be free of misinformation, teacher bias, and emotionally loaded topics. Culture-coded input, both in standardized and teacher-constructed exams, should be taught before it is tested. Culturally conditioned factors in test administration should be carefully considered when an overall judgment of student performance is desired. The test taker who has never experienced a timed, multiple-choice test, should be encouraged to take certain tests more than once. The examiner should be aware of culture-coded test formats in order to avoid those which by their very nature may handicap one linguistic group or another.

References

Alderson, J. Charles, 1978. "The effect of certain methodological variables on cloze test performance and its implications for the use of the cloze procedure in EFL testing." Paper presented at the Fifth International Congress of Applied Linguistics, Montreal.

Condon, Eliane, 1975. "The cultural context of language testing." In *Papers on Language Testing: 1967-1974*, edited by Leslie Palmer and Bernard Spolsky. Washington, D.C.: TESOL.

Croft, Kenneth, 1980. *Readings on English as a Second Language*. Boston: Little, Brown, and Co.

Curt, Carmen Judith, 1984. *Non-Verbal Communication in Puerto Rico*. Cambridge: Evaluation, Dissemination, and Assessment Center.

Goodenough, Ward H., 1979. *Culture, Language and Society*. Menloe Park: Benjamin Cummings Publishers.

Harris, Philip R., and Robert Moran, 1979. *Managing Cultural Differences*. Houston: Gulf Publishing Co.

Kohls, L. Robert, 1981. *Developing Intercultural Awareness*. Washington, D.C.: SIETAR (Society for Intercultural Education, Training, and Research).

Oller, John W., Jr., J. Donald Bowen, Ton That Dien, and Victor Mason, 1972. "Cloze Test in English, Thai, and Vietnamese: native and non-native performance." *Language Learning* 22: 1–15.

Stewart, Edward, 1972. *American Cultural Patterns*. Chicago: Intercultural Press.

The Challenge of a Multicultural Elementary ESL Class: Insights and Suggestions

Linda S. Evans

T HE NUMBER OF CHILDREN entering school for whom English is not a first language has risen dramatically in the last decade and, from all indications, the numbers will continue to increase. While not all of these children are classified as limited English proficient (LEP), English as a second language (ESL) programs have been set up to service the linguistic needs of those who are. The goal of these programs is simple: to provide the students with the skills they need to function successfully in a mainstream classroom. Most programs are designed to teach students listening, speaking, reading, and writing skills. While these skills are certainly central to a student's success in a mainstream classroom, they are not the whole story. The LEP student experiences not only a new language when entering the American public school system, but also a new culture. It is not enough to know how to speak, understand, read, and write English. The student must also learn a new set of rules for functioning in the American culture.

This is no easy task at any level, but it becomes increasingly complex at the elementary school level, where ESL programs exist within a variety of frameworks and the students in the programs often represent a spectrum of different language and cultural groups. How does the ESL teacher approach such a task? Becoming bicultural is vital to the success of the LEP student, but what is culture and can it be taught?

9

To provide a starting point for any discussion about teaching a multicultural class, there should be a clear understanding of what is meant by the term "culture." Culture can be described as "all the aspects of one society; how its people behave, feel and interact" (Donoghue and Kunkle 1979, p. 82). It includes learned behavior patterns, attitudes, and material things (Nine Curt 1976, p. 4). Culture determines such things as how adults and children greet one another, what gestures they employ, how they view the concept of time, their perceptions of authority, and the social relations they develop. These issues operate, for the most part, without awareness (Donoghue and Kunkle 1979, p. 83). These patterns are learned; therefore, if culture is learned, one should be able to teach it (Hall 1973, p. 45).

In the context of a multicultural ESL class, several other questions must be explored. If culture is learned and, therefore, can be taught, how does the ESL teacher go about teaching culture? Furthermore, whose culture should be taught in a multicultural class? Given the time constraints placed on the ESL teacher, are there ways to utilize academic lessons to develop cultural awareness in LEP students? What resources, in both the school and community, can the ESL teacher draw upon?

The answers to these questions will vary according to the framework of each individual ESL program. In order to come to any realistic conclusions, it is important to explore first the nature of ESL programs in the elementary school setting.

ESL PROGRAMS IN THE ELEMENTARY SCHOOL

ESL instruction exists in many forms at the elementary school level. Programs vary according to a number of factors, such as the backgrounds of the students in the district, the philosophy of the administrators and teachers involved in program development, the attitudes of the community, and the wishes of the parents. In general, ESL programs fall into four categories: pull-out programs; programs that serve as a component of a bilingual program; programs that consist of a tutorial situation within a mainstream classroom; and self-contained immersion programs.

The pull-out program consists of a teacher, tutor, or paraprofessional who pulls LEP students out of their mainstream classrooms to attend ESL classes of approximately 30 to 45 minutes in length. A schedule is set in cooperation with the mainstream teacher. The ESL teacher or tutor may see the student every day or several days a week. The amount of communication between an ESL instructor and the classroom teacher varies. In some schools, the ESL instructor is a tutor or paraprofessional who is directed by the classroom teacher as to what content should be covered. In other schools, the tutor or paraprofessional works independently of the classroom teacher, but under the supervision of an ESL program administrator. The ESL teacher is almost always independent of the classroom teacher. However, ESL teachers often try to coordinate their lessons with those in the mainstream classroom in order to reinforce the students' understanding of those concepts.

In a pull-out program, students can be grouped for instruction by grade level or by level of English proficiency. Either way, in a school with a variety of cultural groups, it is likely that the ESL classes will be made up of students from different cultural backgrounds.

An ESL program can also function as a component of a bilingual program. In this situation, it can take several forms. It can be a pull-out from the bilingual class, having many of the attributes outlined above for a pull-out program, or it can be part of the bilingual class, and taught by the bilingual teacher. Since bilingual programs contain children of one linguistic background grouped together for instruction, the ESL class will also be made up of children from similar cultural backgrounds. However, many schools with bilingual programs also have a sampling of children from linguistic groups other than the one addressed by the bilingual program. These children are often placed in mainstream classrooms, but join the students from the bilingual program for ESL instruction from the bilingual teacher. This would increase the potential for a multicultural ESL class.

Another framework within which ESL functions in elementary schools is the mainstream classroom. In this situation, the classroom teacher provides language development activities for the LEP child. This often occurs in schools which have only a few LEP children. The emphasis of the mainstream class is academic. Therefore, it is important for classroom teachers with LEP students to develop techniques for using the reading and content-area materials to cultivate cultural awareness not only in the LEP student, but in the other students as well. If the benefits of this situation are capitalized upon, this can be a very culturally rewarding experience for everyone involved.

While the first three types of ESL programs are the most prevalent in elementary schools, the self-contained ESL class is another alternative. The self-contained classroom is usually a multi-grade, multicultural class in which the mainstream curriculum is adapted to teach language and culture, as well as content-area material. The class size tends to be smaller than in mainstream classes, and instruction is usually more individualized.

Self-contained ESL classes are often found in schools with LEP children from a variety of linguistic backgrounds, ruling out the development of a bilingual class, and where the mainstream classes are large enough to prevent LEP students from getting the individualized instruction they need. In many cases, classroom teachers feel as though they lack the necessary training or skills to provide effective instruction for LEP students. The philosophy behind self-contained ESL programs is that placement of LEP students in a smaller class with a teacher trained in second language acquisition and elementary education will result in speedier acquisition of the English skills needed in a mainstream class.

The result of a self-contained ESL program is a class that encompasses many cultures, many levels, and possibly many grades. In such a situation, the development of multicultural awareness in both teacher and students is not only desirable, but a real necessity.

The issue raised by all the programs described is not whether culture should be an integral part of the ESL class, but rather how teachers in each of the four types of programs can turn the anxiety of being different into the pride of being oneself and enjoying others who are unique (Wallace 1981, p. 89).

Developing Cultural Awareness in the ESL Class

The first step in any program is to get to know the students, paying careful attention to their ethnic origins, personal backgrounds and amount of time they have been in the U.S., prior schooling experiences, ages and grade levels, language abilities in their native language and English, and attitudes toward school and their new environment. That is, the teacher must find out what each student knows (i.e., cultural, language, and academic skills), what is possible (i.e., level of development according to Piaget, Kholberg, Hunt, and others), and what is important (home, family, friends, neighborhood, interests, projects). This process can be described as a kind of "cultural diagnosis" and can prove to be very insightful (Wallace 1981, pp. 89 and 90).

How can a teacher best utilize this cultural diagnosis? Once a teacher has a cultural map of where the students have been and where they are, it is possible to plan a route for where they need to go. To carry the metaphor a bit further, cultural awareness is not a one-way street. It is not enough to teach LEP students about American culture; it is educational negligence to ignore the richness and diversity of experience that exists in a class of individuals from many different cultures.

Helping the students to know and appreciate themselves and their own cultures not only builds self-esteem, but also opens students up to the excitement of learning about the cultures of their classmates, as well as the American culture.

Most teachers lack sufficient time to teach the many concepts that appear in the curriculum. This may be part of the reason why the teaching of culture has been relegated to a secondary status in many ESL classes. Part of the art of teaching is getting as much mileage as possible from every situation in a school day, and culture lends itself very easily to this. Many ESL teachers find it beneficial to supplement the ESL curriculum with content-area materials. This approach forms a natural bridge between what goes on in the ESL class and what the child experiences in the mainstream classroom, while diminishing some of the fragmentation that can take place in the school day. Because it is impossible to escape cultural influence in the subjects of reading, social studies, math, and even science, the challenge for the ESL teacher is to bring this information to consciousness and use it as a starting point for discussion. For example, the stories in basal readers contain a lot of cultural information. A story about a trip to a farm can lead to a discussion about the various types of farms the students have seen, the differences between urban and rural environments, or even the concept of pets versus farm animals and how animals are perceived in the students' native cultures.

The teacher should be aware that certain pictures or topics might cause confusion. If a reading series was developed in a northern region, for example, there might be references to things that would be unfamiliar to students from a southern or tropical climate. The concept of a fall with leaves that change colors and have to be raked, or a winter with snow that can be made into snowmen or shoveled off sidewalks might be very foreign to some of the students. The point, however, is not to avoid such topics, but rather to help students understand them by linking them to familiar experiences. A teacher could use a picture of a snowman to reinforce the initial consonant *s*, but it might be better to introduce this sound using a picture of sand on a beach or a sandal like those worn in the students' native country. Then, when the picture of the snowman is used, the teacher and students can talk about the concept of snow, cold winters, what people do in the north, etc. Academic subject matter is being taught, and cultural information is being shared. It may lengthen the reading lesson a bit, but it is more efficient and meaningful than planning separate lessons for reading and culture.

Social studies lessons are natural vehicles for the development of cultural awareness. When teachers discuss the surrounding community, city, state, or region, and specific topics such as jobs, homes, or events, the students can make a comparison with their own backgrounds and origins. Once a teacher establishes an environment of sharing and exploring cultural differences during academic lessons, students will begin to pick up on issues that relate to their backgrounds and won't wait to be asked for information about their native cultures.

In addition to traditional academic subjects, other areas of the curriculum can be used to develop cultural awareness. The arts provide an excellent and highly motivating opportunity to learn about other cultures. The children can share music, dance, folklore, and storytelling from their native cultures. Some ESL teachers have a regular storytelling time, when students can tell stories that their parents or grandparents have told them, or make up stories of their own. Other teachers have a "story corner," in which students can read or tell stories into a tape recorder; these stories can then be shared with the class later.

Pantomime and puppetry are popular in cultures around the world, and are an exciting vehicle for cultural sharing. Pantomime allows students to become more aware of how they use their bodies to express ideas and feelings, and encourages students to try out new ways of moving and communicating. Puppetry provides an opportunity for students to use English without the intimidation that can come from being exposed to the entire class.

Games are a fun way to share one's culture. All cultures seem to have games that children learn; some use paper and pencil, others are board games, and still others are played on the playground. Many children will voluntarily share their games, but others have to be coaxed. American playground games such as jump-rope jingles and song/action games are an excellent source of language development activities.

In addition to teaching academic skills and promoting cultural awareness, the arts serve another important function. Imagine the LEP child who spends a large percentage of his or her time in school feeling confused and unable to understand what is happening. To have an entire class show interest in something from his or her native culture (such as a game, dance, or art form) legitimizes that child's culture as interesting and viable, and gives the child's self-esteem a tremendous boost. Given the importance of self-esteem and motivation in the learning process, this benefit cannot be stressed enough.

Culture does not have to be separated from the regular activities of an ESL or mainstream class or put under a spotlight to be taught effectively. Both the native cultures of the students and the American culture can be brought to consciousness and taught simply by approaching the daily lessons with an awareness of how culture permeates all that is done in a school day.

CULTURAL RESOURCES OUTSIDE THE ESL CLASSROOM

Up to this point an effort has been made to emphasize the wealth of cultural information that can be found within the walls of an ESL classroom. Often teachers feel insecure in dealing with LEP children because they assume that to be effective teachers they must be the reservoir from which all learning is taken. Actually, the most effective teachers are those who are able to involve the students in the learning process to the point where the teacher and the students are gaining knowledge from each other. Successful teachers do more than impart knowledge; they manage and facilitate the sharing of knowledge within a class.

In addition to making use of cultural information that can be found within a classroom, ESL teachers can draw on a number of other school resources. Specialists in the areas of media, art, music, and drama are often very willing to cooperate on cultural projects. Media specialists can direct children to books about a variety of cultures. They are also often willing to follow a teacher's request about a particular book to read aloud to the class during their library period. In addition, media specialists have access to films, filmstrips, and records that deal with cultural information.

Art specialists can provide techniques and guidance to teachers who would like to organize a class art project on a certain theme. While numerous art classes are devoted to seasonal projects, many art specialists are open to cultural diversity in the spectrum of projects chosen. For example, at Christmastime children often make tree ornaments or candles. To add diversity, the children could also be taught to make a "God's Eye" or "ojo de Dios," a symbol used in much of Latin America to watch over the children and protect them from evil. For the new year, projects dealing with Chinese New Year might be appropriate for a class with Chinese or Vietnamese students.

Music specialists can introduce children to songs from other cultures. An effort could be made to include songs and dances from cultures represented in the school as part of the annual pageants or music programs. If the music specialist is interested but doesn't have the necessary materials, the ESL or classroom teacher could approach parents for traditional songs from their native countries.

The drama specialist often works hand-in-hand with the music specialist. Drama can supply the students with a non-threatening way to try out some of the cultural information they have learned and to experiment with different gestures and actions. It is non-threatening because the student is taking on a different character, "wearing a mask," and thus not representing himself at all. Drama specialists might also be able to provide the ESL teacher with hints on using drama in the ESL class.

In addition to the school specialists, ESL or classroom teachers may be able to draw on the insights and talents of other staff members in providing cultural experiences for the students. Many staffs include bilingual/bicultural individuals as teachers, instructional aides, administrators, and support staff, such as cafeteria and custodial workers. Even if these staff members do not work directly with the LEP students, the ESL teacher can use them as information sources, sounding boards, and role models for the students. They may also be able to provide translation services and, even more important, a link between the school and the students' home.

One school resource that should not be overlooked is the other students. Peer involvement can provide many of the same benefits as staff involvement, in addition to giving younger students the advantage of seeing older students who might have had the same insecurities they are experiencing now. It is important to choose carefully when using peer involvement, but a good choice can provide an LEP student with a salient image of someone who has achieved a measure of success in another culture.

Outside resources need not stop at the school yard gate. Unfortunately, many schools seem to function as entities separate from the surrounding communities. This may be more true in large cities or in communities where busing has done away with the neighborhood school, but it does not mean that the community is of no value to the school. There are often cultural resources within walking distance of the school—cultural organizations, public libraries, museums or exhibits, and professionals in the community from diverse cultural backgrounds. Most of these resources are free and easily accessible once contact has been made. Some organizations may even be willing to send representatives to the school so that a larger number of students can profit from the experience.

The school can also be a cultural resource to the community. Every day ESL, bilingual, and classroom teachers are engaged in innovative cultural activities with their students. A call to the local newspaper or television station is usually welcome, as reporters and news people are generally eager to find out what is going on in the schools. Using the local media to show a community that cultural awareness is being cultivated in the schools can have a positive impact on the community's image of students and families from different cultural backgrounds.

In summary, the teaching of culture in a multicultural ESL class should not be an extraneous or secondary goal in the curriculum. The ESL class is a place for LEP students to learn the skills, academic and cultural, that they will need to become successful and fulfilled students and members of their new culture. Therefore, the teacher of a multicultural elementary ESL class is challenged to capitalize on the cultural diversity in the class, school, and community to nurture in the students an awareness of and excitement about not only the American culture, but also their own cultures, and those of their classmates.

A teacher's ability to meet this challenge will depend on how well he or she utilizes the available resources. An ESL or classroom teacher who is interested in promoting multicultural exploration in a class should:

1. Analyze the ESL services provided in the school. Knowing the nature of the program and its components can assist the teacher in structuring a realistic cultural component.

2. Perform a "cultural diagnosis" on the class. This helps the teacher get to know the students' ethnic, personal, and academic backgrounds, their native and English language abilities, and their attitudes and motivation.

3. Look for ways to include culture in academic lessons. Approaching the lesson with a critical eye for cultural information could head off confusion on the part of the students and serve as a springboard for further discussions.

4. Emphasize not only the American culture, but also the native cultures of the students in the class. Learning culture is a two-way street, and students will learn better if they have something in their own experience to which they can relate the new knowledge.

5. Use the arts to promote cultural understanding and awareness. This produces a highly motivating learning environment and builds self-esteem in the students.

6. Utilize human resources within the school when appropriate. Specialists, staff members, and other students are excellent sources of information, project support, and role models.

7. Utilize the community resources that are available. Cultural organizations, public libraries, museums, and professionals in the community from various cultural backgrounds are often convenient to the school and available at no charge or for a nominal fee.

8. Develop an atmosphere of cultural exploration and acceptance in the classroom so that the anxiety of being different is turned into the pride of being oneself and enjoying others who are unique.

RESOURCES FOR TEACHERS OF MULTICULTURAL ESL CLASSES

General

Ashworth, Mary, and Patricia Wakefield, 1982. *Teaching the Non-English-Speaking Child: Grades K-2.* Washington, D.C.: Center for Applied Linguistics.

Banks, James A., 1979. *Teaching Strategies for Ethnic Studies.* 2nd ed. Boston: Allyn and Bacon.

Cortes, Carlos, 1976. *Understanding You and Them: Tips for Teaching About Ethnicity.* Boulder, CO: ERIC Clearinghouse for Social Studies.

Kendon, Adam, 1981. *Non-Verbal Communication, Interaction, and Gesture.* The Hague: Mouton Publishers.

King, Edith W., 1980. *Teaching Ethnic Awareness: Methods and Materials for the Elementary School.* Santa Monica, CA: Goodyear Publishing Company, Inc.

Nine Curt, Judith Carmen, 1979. *Non-Verbal Communication.* Cambridge, MA: National Assessment and Dissemination Center.

Culture Through the Arts

Storytelling:

Briggs, Nancy E., and Joseph A. Wagner, 1970. *Children's Literature Through Storytelling and Drama.* Dubuque, IA: Wm. C. Brown Company.

Chambers, Dewey W., 1970. *Storytelling and Creative Drama.* Dubuque, IA: Wm. C. Brown Company.

Lee, F. H., 1946. *Folk Tales of All Nations.* New York: Tudor Publishing Company.

Ziskind, Sylvia, 1976. *Telling Stories to Children.* New York: H. W. Wilson Company.

Puppetry:

Adair, Margaret Weeks, and Elizabeth Patapoff, 1972. *Folk Puppet Plays for the Social Studies.* New York: John Day Company.

Hopper, Grizella H., 1966. *Puppet Making Through the Grades.* Worcester, MA: Davis Publishers, Inc.

Tichenor, Tom, 1959. *Folk Plays for Puppets You Can Make.* New York: Abingdon Press.

Pantomime:

Kipnis, Claude, 1974. *The Mime Book.* New York: Harper and Row, Inc.

Mander, Raymond, 1973. *Pantomime: A Story in Pictures.* New York: Taplinger Publishing Company.

Music:

Graham, Carolyn, 1979. *Jazz Chants for Children.* New York: Oxford University Press.

Kind, Uwe, 1980. *Tune in to English.* New York: Regents Publishing Company.

National Public Radio, 1981. *Music in a New World.* Washington, D.C.: National Public Radio Education Services.

REFERENCES

Castaneda, Alfredo, Richard L. James, and Webster Robbins, 1974. *The Educational Needs of Minority Groups.* Lincoln, NE: Professional Educators Publishers, Inc.

Donoghue, Mildred R., and John F. Kunkle, 1979. *Second Languages in Primary Education.* Rowley, MA: Newbury House Publishers, Inc.

Evans, Linda A., 1982. *Tell Me a Story: Storytelling and Oral Language Development in an ESL Classroom.* Unpublished thesis, Boston University.

Hall, Edward T., 1973. *The Silent Language.* Garden City, NY: Anchor Press.

King, Edith W., 1980. *Teaching Ethnic Awareness: Methods and Materials for the Elementary School.* Santa Monica, CA: Goodyear Publishing Company, Inc.

Nine Curt, Judith Carmen, 1976. *Non-Verbal Communication.* Cambridge, MA: National Assessment and Dissemination Center for Bilingual/Bicultural Education.

Nine Curt, Judith Carmen, 1976. *Teacher Training Pack for a Course on Cultural Awareness.* Cambridge, MA: National Assessment and Dissemination Center for Bilingual/Bicultural Education.

Trueba, Henry T., and Carol Barnett-Mizrahi (eds.), 1981. *Bilingual Multicultural Education and the Professional.* Rowley, MA: Newbury House Publishers, Inc.

Wallace, George N., 1981. "Cultural Awareness: Interaction of Teachers, Parents and Students." In *Perspectives in Multicultural Education,* edited by William E. Sims and Bernice Bass de Martinez. Washington, D.C.: University Press of America, Inc.

Cross-Cultural Coping: Suggestions for Anglo Teachers of ESL to Native Americans

KATHERINE RICHMOND

W HAT DO YOU THINK of when you hear the word *culture*? Refinement? Tradition? Manners? Culture means many things to many people—in fact, some people have collected between 200 and 450 definitions! On one hand, it is possible to define culture simply and somewhat comprehensively as a human society's standards of verbal and nonverbal communication that define a range of behavior acceptable in that society. On the other hand, so defined, culture deeply affects the expectations people hold of themselves and others personally, socially, and professionally, and the responses they make to others as well.

As an ESL teacher, how would you respond to the following situations?

1. A student makes very little eye contact with you.

The author would like to express her thanks to Edwina Hoffman of the Bilingual Education South Eastern Support Center in Miami, to Susan Greenbaum of the University of South Florida, and to Kim Neubauer of the Peace Corps Office of Staging for their personal reflections and input. Thanks are also extended to Thallis Lewis, Director of Bilingual Education, Mississippi Band of Choctaws, Philadelphia, Mississippi, for sharing her experience and suggestions, and to Al Lowe of the University of South Florida for encouragement and research support. Particular gratitude is expressed to the Peace Corps Office of Staging for permission to adapt and use suggested coping strategies.

2. Your students are consistently so soft-spoken that you wonder if the rest of the students can hear when they recite.

3. An infraction of the rules has occurred, which you consider to be quite serious. In order to impress upon your students the seriousness of the situation, you raise your voice. This seems, however, only to make the situation worse.

4. You sense that something is not quite right in your teaching situation. However, nobody—administrator, colleague, or community member—has said anything directly to you about it.

Typically, the responses of an Anglo teacher to these situations might include the following:

1. I bet that child is shy—or else hiding something.

2. I wish they'd speak up! *or* What's the matter, don't they know the answer?

3. Don't they realize how serious this matter is? Don't they care?

4. What's going wrong? If something's the matter, let's get to the point about it.

In many areas of Anglo-American culture, these responses would not only be typical, they might also be productive in terms of beginning to solve the problem. In some native American cultures, however, the responses would be unproductive, and some of the situations would not necessarily be problematic (unless they were misinterpreted by an Anglo teacher). Both the situations and responses are products of culture. When the cultures of the students and their teachers differ, as they do in this case, communication problems may occur.

Behavioral Expectations: The Products of Culture

Culture produces both typical ways of behaving and typical expectations concerning others' behavior. When one person's expectations and another's behavior match, understanding occurs. When they differ, misunderstandings may occur on either side or both. For example, Anglo teachers usually expect to give and receive a good deal of eye contact with students. They expect to project their voices in the classroom, and expect that their students will do so as well. They also usually expect to confront problems directly. In Choctaw culture, however, it is impolite for a child to look a teacher in the eye. Choctaws also speak more softly than their Anglo counterparts, and view raising the voice as a lack of self-control. Criticism or direct verbal confrontation is considered rude.

When people from two different cultures are aware of areas in which cultural signals may differ, they are not as likely to misread each other. If potential misunderstandings are not recognized, however, incidents of miscommunication may accumulate until they become emotional issues. In the case of misunderstandings between students and teachers, the damage is twofold. First, the teacher's personal and professional discomfort often grows to the point where it contributes to the miscommunication. No longer are misunderstandings isolated instances to be shaken off. Instead, they may produce feelings of tension, alienation, unworthiness, isolation, or inadequacy. These may in turn produce more unproductive behavior on the teacher's part, and the problem can snowball. Second, the miscommunication and resultant turmoil may actually interfere with the students' learning.

The purpose of this article is to outline some areas in which cultural misunderstandings may occur between Anglo teachers and native American students, to help teachers recognize signs of culture-related difficulties, and to suggest some practical ways for teachers to cope with these problems. While many of the suggestions in this paper will be related specifically to the Mississippi Choctaw culture, issues raised may provide food for thought concerning other native American groups.

WHERE DO MISUNDERSTANDINGS OCCUR?

Basically, misunderstandings occur in two areas: expectations and responses. By holding certain expectations about classroom interaction, Anglo-American teachers may inadvertently be asking native American children to violate deeply ingrained patterns of communication. When the students do not respond in expected ways, teachers may become frustrated or impatient. For example, Anglo teachers usually expect to be looked in the eye by children who are being reprimanded. Viewing a child's failure to maintain eye contact as a sign of defiance, they are apt to become annoyed when native American children, not wishing to seem impertinent, avert their eyes. The reverse is also true. Native American students may have certain expectations of appropriate adult or teacher behavior that are different from what Anglo teachers have learned. When their expectations are not met, as when teachers raise their voices, students may feel confused, frustrated, tense, or disliked by the teacher.

All teachers want their students to do their best. In an Anglo-oriented society, one's best is usually shown by one's *individual* work—accomplished alone and often in competition with one's peers. However, strongly group-oriented native American children are often more comfortable with a cooperative, non-critical group effort in which the student's personal best is oriented toward a group goal. Individual recitation, too, may pose barriers. For one thing, blunt, direct questioning is usually avoided by native Americans, as is the blunt, public feedback that often follows such recitation. Being put on the spot in front of one's peers may be in conflict with many children's home training. At home, they quietly observe the skills they are to learn, practice them by doing as much as they can with an adult there to watch and help, and then demonstrate them when they are reasonably certain of success. Furthermore, if the children's native language is not English, recitation is complicated by their having to perform individually and publicly in an unfamiliar language on a task they may not have understood.

Occasionally problems occur when materials are used that are appropriate in Anglo culture but not among traditional native Americans. For example, an owl is a symbol of friendly wisdom in many Anglo classrooms. Among traditional Choctaws, the owl is a symbol of death. Likewise, snakes are considered evil omens. However, issues over which cultural misunderstandings occur in the classroom—such as eye contact and individualism—are more often the products of differing viewpoints concerning what is respectful (or respectable) and responsible behavior on the part of both students and teachers.

Another possible area of misunderstanding is the matter of punctuality. In Anglo culture, tasks are governed by the clock: they are begun and finished at the appointed time; perhaps sooner, but certainly no later. In native American culture, time may be governed more by the beginning and completion of the task at hand than by the clock. The task may not be started precisely "on time," but neither will the ending time be dictated by the concept of "closing time."

Classroom seating arrangements provide an excellent example of expectations for student and teacher behavior. A common arrangement in Anglo classrooms involves individuals seated row-by-row, with the teacher standing at the front exercising a directive form of leadership. "Classroom control" may include such behaviors as strong projection of voice, sustained eye contact from a standing position, obvious displays of enthusiasm or displeasure, and public comments (questions, praise, challenge, reprimand) directed to individuals. On the other hand, native American children may do better (at least initially) seated in small groups or committees. Not only are the small groups more comfortable in terms of group effort, but they also provide for the more egalitarian treatment of children expected by many native American children and parents. This treatment includes allowing children to take reasonable responsibility for the well-being of the group as well as for their own individual actions.

Group seating also allows a teacher to instruct native American children in a manner which is culturally familiar to them: sitting with the children at their own eye level, speaking softly, maintaining a calm demeanor, demonstrating skills, and supporting the children as they practice. Demonstration of tasks is particularly important, not only because it is culturally familiar, but because it capitalizes on strengths in visual and auditory memory. Moreover, demonstrating tasks gives limited English proficient children the chance not only to understand the task they are supposed to be doing, but also to develop English language concepts at the same time.

RECOGNIZING CULTURE-RELATED PROBLEMS[1]

In Oneself

To a greater or lesser degree, it is normal to experience some conflict when living and interacting in another culture. However, people react in different ways to being in a new situation. Some people become depressed, perhaps withdrawing from the people of the new culture and having little energy left for doing anything that requires much mental or physical effort. They are uncomfortable and may blame people from the new culture for their discomfort. Other people look for similarities to their own culture and rely upon these similarities for support. Participation in familiar activities, such as sports or reading, may help preserve a person's sense of identity and can help a person get over a period of initial adjustment. However, this can also become an escape mechanism, leading to avoidance of people from the new culture and situations which are potentially uncomfortable.

Peace Corps volunteers are trained to look for certain signs that may indicate cultural adjustment problems. An adaptation of these warning signs may be helpful to Anglo teachers residing and/or working on Indian reservations:

1. Longing for certain foods or personal comforts not readily obtainable on the reservation.

2. Reluctance to be with native Americans except in highly structured situations.

---

1. Much of the material pertaining to recognizing and coping with culture-related problems has been adapted from B. Barger and J. Hogan, 1982. *Center for Reassessment and Training*. Washington, DC: Peace Corps Office of Staging, 78-82. Adapted by permission of the Peace Corps Office of Staging.

3. Associating mostly (or exclusively) with non-Indians.

4. Finding oneself talking about native Americans as "them" or "these people" and blaming them for problems in professional or personal relationships.

5. Spending more time than usual drinking (especially excessively), sleeping, eating, bathing, grooming oneself, daydreaming, playing cards (especially solitaire), reading, organizing or reorganizing one's personal belongings.

In One's Students

How can a teacher tell when a cross-cultural misunderstanding is interfering with the instructional process? Sometimes the behavior of the students may give a clue. Indications of problems include:

1. *Non-compliance.* Students may not verbalize any protest; they simply may not do what has been asked of them if the request violates deeply held values or customary behavior.

2. *Silence,* particularly in response to a blunt or culturally inappropriate question.

3. *"I don't know."* A response of "I don't know" may mean "I don't want to tell you."

4. *Interrupting.* This may indicate that students are misreading conversational signals, not that they are trying to be rude.

5. *Talking in shorter sentences than normal,* particularly when giving individual responses to questions.

6. *Answering questions chorally, rather than individually, or giving answers to other students in the native language.* These problems are often the result of native American students' preference for working together rather than being "put on the spot" or expected to compete against or criticize other individuals.

COPING WITH CULTURE-RELATED PROBLEMS

The first step in dealing with problems resulting from cultural dissonance is simply to recognize that you are having problems and that you have certain feelings. If you recognize your feelings, you can often see what you need to do to overcome both your feelings and any underlying difficulties in communication. It is hard to do anything when you feel uncomfortable, but the only thing that will really help is to recognize your own needs and the needs of your students and to find culturally appropriate ways of dealing with them.

Learning as much as you can about the local culture will help to prevent some of your problems. For example, it can be reassuring to know that it is not considered polite in Choctaw culture for children to look directly at their teacher. The lack of eye contact is not intended to show dislike, disinterest, or defiance. When in doubt about the appropriateness or acceptability of your own actions, ask a colleague. Remember to convey that you are asking out of concern for the children and their learning, and to present your need for information tactfully and in a way that communicates your respect for native American culture. Also, since people's viewpoints are colored by their own experiences, it may be helpful to get more than one person's point of view.

Patiently observing other people's interactions also helps, particularly in the area of feedback, or learning how one's actions are being perceived by others. Feedback, however, is culturally influenced both in the way it is given and in the way it is interpreted. It takes a while to learn to interpret communicative signals. If direct confrontation and criticism are considered impolite, the feedback you get will probably be indirect and quite subtle. Learn to recognize unspoken signals that something has gone wrong in your interaction. Just as important, learn to recognize the signs that things are going well, that you are liked and appreciated. Try to learn, too, what signals do not mean. For example, Choctaw children may not show much excitement over compliments or gifts. That doesn't mean that they are not appreciative of you or your gesture—they simply don't express emotion the way majority-culture children might.

When you are unsure of the appropriateness of your behavior or the meaning of feedback, you may observe and imitate others' actions. While this is one way of learning culturally acceptable behaviors, it can be carried to an extreme that is unnatural or out of character for you. As a result, you may appear ridiculous, insincere, and offensive. You are the product of your culture, just as your students, their families, and your colleagues are the products of theirs. All of you need to be yourselves, not someone else. You cannot adopt a new cultural identity in a few days or weeks; to imply that you can is to insult an old and very rich cultural heritage which has taken centuries to form. Do watch others interact—see what kind of feedback they give each other. Try to modify your own expectations to fit your situation, and be sensitive to the responses your behavior may evoke. But don't try to be anyone but yourself.

Practical Suggestions for Teachers

While some of these suggestions are specifically oriented to working with Mississippi Choctaw children, they may raise valuable questions in the minds of teachers working with other groups.

1. Remember that you are the guest on the reservation and that your hosts have a right to let their cultural patterns predominate.

2. Learn as much of the Choctaw language (and culture) as you can. As the French proverb states, "The person who speaks two languages is worth two." And, from a purely practical standpoint, about 70% of Choctaw families speak Choctaw exclusively at home.

3. Encourage the children to be proud of their heritage and of their language. Be yourself—but also learn from your students.

4. Approach questions with the goal of learning and doing what will be best for the students.

5. Participate in community activities, such as sporting events, that are open to the public. Some traditional ceremonies or activities will be for tribe members only, but at others your attendance will be welcome.

6. Talk to successful teachers and paraprofessionals—especially Choctaws—for suggestions on what techniques have worked for them.

7. If you have Choctaw teachers or paraprofessionals in your classroom, learn as much as you can from watching their interactions with the students. Pay special attention to where they sit or stand, to their tone of voice, to how they address the students and to how they present the subject matter.

8. Don't raise your voice. In Anglo culture, this may indicate either enthusiasm or seriousness of purpose. In Choctaw culture, it indicates a lack of self-control.

9. "Classroom control" does not mean dominating the classroom. Nondirective leadership is part of Choctaw culture. One way to implement this is to form classroom committees that participate in the rule-making and decision-making process—and take responsibility for their actions. Also, remember that children everywhere sometimes "act up" simply because they want a little personal attention.

10. Try to remember that lack of eye contact is a sign of respect—not of disinterest.

11. You may be used to seeing a lot of excitement on the part of majority-culture children. Choctaw children don't display as much excitement, but that doesn't mean that they are not interested or that they dislike you.

12. Avoid direct confrontation and public criticism. They are considered rude in Choctaw culture.

13. Be sensitive to differences between the Choctaw and English languages. Some of the English sounds don't exist in Choctaw, and Choctaw has some sounds that don't exist in American English. Also, Choctaw doesn't have as many multiple-meaning words as English does, and doesn't form plurals the way English does.

14. Remember that children who have lived off the reservation for a while may be more proficient in English than your other students. As a result, they may be bored. Try to adapt your instruction to make some provision for these children, too.

15. Keep in mind that family obligations can include both extended family and close friends. If one of your students has a death in the family, for example, his or her friends may also be absent from school.

16. Be sensitive to traditional beliefs or taboos. For example, an owl may represent wisdom in Anglo culture. In traditional Choctaw culture, it represents death. Snakes, among traditional Choctaw children, are also considered evil omens.

17. When asking questions, remember that most of your students are responding in a second language, therefore, they may respond slowly. Give them time—and never make fun of a response.

18. Bear in mind that it is courteous and respectful in Choctaw culture to pause and weigh one's words before responding to a question or comment. Your children may need this time but not know how to communicate that need to you. Allow plenty of time when children are responding; don't be quick to jump in with a comment or to call on another child. (Try counting to five slowly and then see what's happening with the students.)

19. It is best not to tease or joke with your students until you know them well. You may be misunderstood.

20. It is usually more effective to seat the children in small groups or committees. Seating them row by row doesn't work. And remember to build some teamwork into your lesson plans.

21. Don't expect children to volunteer for answers or tasks. Choctaw children usually won't.

22. It is better to handle discipline yourself than to send a child to the principal. It is much more effective to give the children choices within firm guidelines and to let them take some responsibility for disciplining themselves. Never resort to yelling, begging, or embarrassing a child. It is particularly ineffective to make a child stand in the corner.

23. Avoid making comments that would discourage a child about his or her own learning capabilities—especially in public.

24. While Anglo culture places a great value on getting right to the point, it is more appropriate in Choctaw culture to chat with a person first and then to ask necessary questions in an indirect way.

25. Sit with the children while demonstrating a task to them; then let them try it, practice, and then show you the results of their efforts.

26. Use a lot of visuals and manipulatives—and make sure they are culturally appropriate.

27. Try to remember that time may be perceived in relationship to the task rather than the clock.

28. Be patient in developing relationships. Time and respect are absolutely necessary.

29. Remember that Choctaw children are like children everywhere. They need love, understanding, respect, and patience in order to learn. Part of your job is to find ways to communicate these things to them in ways that they will understand. Ask yourself how you can adapt or modify your teaching behaviors in order to communicate most effectively with your students and their families.

REFERENCES

Barger, B., and J. Hogan, 1982. *Center for Reassessment and Training* (Peace Corps Training Manual). Washington, D.C.: Peace Corps Office of Staging.
Blanchard, K., 1981. *The Mississippi Choctaws at Play: The Serious Side of Leisure.* Urbana, IL: The University of Illinois Press.

Brod, R.L., 1979. *Choctaw Education*. Box Elder, MT: LPS & Associates (ERIC Document Reproduction Service No. 197 920).

Croft, K., 1980. "The Matter of Culture." In *Readings on English as a Second Language*, 2nd ed., edited by K. Croft, 531–538. Cambridge, MA: Winthrop Publishers, Inc.

Greenbaum, P., 1985. "Nonverbal Differences in Communication Style Between American Indian and Anglo Elementary Classrooms." *American Educational Research Journal* 22, 1: 101–115.

Greenbaum, P., and S. Greenbaum, 1983. "Cultural Differences, Nonverbal Regulation, and Classroom Interaction: Sociolinguistic Interference in American Indian Education." *Peabody Journal of Education* 61, 1: 16–33.

Greenbaum, S., and P. Greenbaum, 1984. "Integrating Ethnographic and Quantitative Research: A Reply to Kleinfeld with Implications for American Indian Self-determination." *Anthropology and Education Quarterly* 15, 2: 171–173.

Kleinfeld, J., G.W. McDiarmid, S. Grubis, and W. Parrett, 1983. "Doing Research on Effective Cross-Cultural Teaching: The Teacher Tale." *Peabody Journal of Education* 61, 1: 86–106.

Levine, D., and M. Adelman, 1982. *Beyond Language: Intercultural Communication for English as a Second Language*. Englewood Cliffs, NJ: Prentice-Hall, Inc.

McKee, J.O., and J.A. Schlenker, 1980. *The Choctaws: Cultural Evolution of a Native American Tribe*. Jackson, MS: University Press of Mississippi.

Peterson, J.P., 1975. "The Teacher as Learner: A Year with the Choctaws." *Journal of Applied Communications Research* 3, 1: 1–7.

Trifanovitch, G., 1980. "Culture Learning/Culture Teaching." In *Readings on English as a Second Language*, 2nd ed., edited by K. Croft, 550–558. Cambridge, MA: Winthrop Publishers, Inc.

White, R., 1983. *The Roots of Dependency: Subsistence, Environment, and Social Change Among the Choctaws, Pawnees, and Navajos*. Lincoln, NE: University of Nebraska Press.

Some Intercultural Aspects of ESL Instruction for Pre-Literates

Roger W. Cole

IN THE PERIOD from 1980 to 1982, the state of Florida witnessed an enormous influx of Cuban and Haitian refugees or entrants as a result of the Mariel Boatlift and political and economic conditions in Haiti. Florida social service agencies were confronted with a large population of adult entrants with minimal or no functional English language skills, limited or no educational backgrounds, and, in the case of the Haitians, a lack of literacy in any language. Existing public and private educational programs designed to provide ESL instruction had had little experience with such populations in the past, despite influxes of Southeast Asian refugees in the 1970s. Instead, existing programs had focused upon the non-adult population (various migrant programs and bilingual/ESOL K-12 programs), or the non-head-of-household adults (Indo-Chinese refugee programs, adult education, etc.). Unfortunately, the necessity of gainful employment for heads-of-households generally prevents or discourages them from participating in conventionally delivered ESL programs.

Yet ironically, this segment of the entrant population—heads-of-households (particularly males)—is most in need of functional ESL skills precisely because such skills enhance employability. Moreover, the assumptions, organization, and curricula of conventional ESL programs were not designed to address the specific cultural, psychological, and socioeconomic problems of many Cuban and Haitian

33

entrants. Their lack of educational and/or vocational training and low levels of literacy rendered them incapable of benefiting from such programs. The assimilation of such populations into a highly verbal and literate English-speaking society and marketplace, therefore, poses enormous obstacles for educational and social service agencies. From the ESL standpoint, even "Survival English" programs (Smith 1987) are of limited applicability for such populations because:

1. Participants most in need of survival English generally lack the requisite basic educational background or even the first language literacy necessary to benefit from conventional programs.

2. Participants need survival English much more rapidly than conventional programs are designed to deliver it.

3. Participants most in need of survival English are generally (of necessity) employed or seeking employment and are thereby prevented from participating because of work-related conflicts.

4. Participants represent a population with high attrition in educational and/or training programs; therefore, even if they begin a program, the English training may not be rapid or intensive enough for any lasting benefit before the participant drops out.

5. The materials, teaching methodologies, and content of conventional ESL programs are generally irrelevant to participant needs, and, in themselves, may contribute to high attrition.

In 1982, the author competed for and was awarded a grant to mount a pilot ESL project under the auspices of the Cuban-Haitian Entrants Social Services (CHESS) division of the Hillsborough County (Florida) Division of Health and Rehabilitative Services. The proposal succeeded, in some measure, because it analyzed the problem in the manner outlined in the preceding paragraphs; that is, cultural considerations were foremost.

PROJECT DESCRIPTION

The ESL project was designed to provide a rapid, intensive survival-level program in English whose content emphasized pre-vocational communication skills and home management information (defined below). The target population was approximately 150 Cuban and Haitian entrants referred to the program by the county. This population was adult, primarily male, with little or no functional ability (speaking, reading, writing, or understanding) in English, and generally uneducated or functionally illiterate even in their native tongues.

The project goals were, therefore:

- to provide participants with the minimum listening comprehension abilities in English necessary for (1) entry-level employment (or retention), (2) vocational training with further ESL, and (3) limited social interaction.

- to provide participants with the minimum speaking ability necessary for the same.

- to provide participants who already enjoyed some measure of literacy in their first language(s) with a minimum ability to read the English appropriate for continued training (vocational-with-ELS) and/or entry-level employment; or, to provide participants not literate in any tongue the basic foundation to become literate in English through further education.

- to provide participants with useful information and skills in order to assist them in sociocultural adjustment, particularly in the area of home management and pre-vocational processes.

The first three of these goals were inspired by Mary Galvan (1982) and Jeanne Lopez-Valadez (1982), and other proponents of "Bilingual Vocational Education." (See Joan Friedenberg and Curtis Bradley's *The Vocational ESL Handbook* [Rowley, MA: Newbury House, 1981] for a further discussion of Bilingual Vocational Education programs.) Galvan and others strongly reject the conventional notion that high-level, or even intermediate-level, functional ESL ability is a prerequisite to vocational training or education. Instead, they offer convincing evidence that students and trainees with even the most limited English skills can successfully complete vocational training, provided they are placed in well-designed bilingual vocational educational programs. In fact, Galvan argues that their success in vocational training is generally the cause or occasion for the improvement of their ESL skills, and not the opposite, as is generally supposed.

Consonant with these arguments, we negotiated agreements with a nearby vocational educational institution to accept participants who completed our program for continued vocational-ESL training. The fourth goal was inspired by a mounting body of theory and research tending to show that English, or any other language, is best acquired not as an object in itself, but as a tool or medium for learning something else, such as a vocation. (See, for example, Saville-Troike 1976.)

To accomplish these goals, three groups of 50 students each were enrolled in one of three consecutive nine-week sessions. Each session provided three hours of intensive pre-vocational ESL instruction each evening (6:30 to 9:30 P.M.), four days per week (Monday through Wednesday, plus Friday). The Thursday evening session each week was devoted exclusively to the home management content. A total of 150 participants were thus entered between March and October 1982. The use of nine-week sessions permitted three entry points for referrals during the course of the project.

Essentially two levels were established:

Level 1:   Virtually no English and no literacy in the native language.

Level 2:   Limited English plus some degree of literacy in the native language.

Participants in Level 2 were referred to bilingual vocational programs or employers upon satisfactory completion. Participants initially assigned to Level 1 were either (a) moved to Level 2 on completion, (b) referred to employers if continuation was not possible, or (c) referred to bilingual vocational or other adult education programs if progress warranted.

CURRICULUM AND INSTRUCTION

Placement and other testing was a major procedural question owing to the inapplicability of most widely used standardized tests of English (TOEFL, CELT, etc.), all of which assume literacy. However, since 1980, in response to precisely this problem with respect to refugees, a number of "oral interview" instruments have been developed and used, including the BVOPT, (*Bilingual Vocational Oral Proficiency Test*), which we selected.[1] The BVOPT was selected because of its vocational orientation and its structure; it consists of an informal initial interview, a specific questions section, and a picture stimulus free-response section.

The BVOPT requires no reading or writing; students are given instructions in their native tongues by administrators or aides. Any section of the test is terminated when a student has reached a proficiency plateau (or demonstrates undue frustration); therefore, the student participates in and leaves the process with a feeling of success rather than anxiety. Different forms of the same test allow it to be used both for initial placement and for an exit evaluation of progress. An important consideration for us was that the reliability and validity

---

1. The BVOPT was developed by Mary Galvan and published by Melton Peninsula (Dallas, TX; 1981). Other oral testing instruments include the IOI *(Ilyin Oral Interview)* by Donna Ilyin (Rowley, MA: Newbury House); and the BEST *(Basic English Skills Test)* developed by the Center for Applied Linguistics.

norms published for the test were confirmed by our experience in using it. It also offered ease of administration and test-anxiety reduction for the participants.

Teaching materials included some published materials, and a considerable body constructed by the staff in the preservice workshops. Published materials developed by Delta Systems for survival-level English, especially for students with little or no educational background, were found to be particularly useful.

Preservice workshops for the staff, in addition to work on curriculum and materials for instruction, also provided a strong cultural component. This cultural component included information about the native languages of the participants (Cuban Spanish and Haitian Creole); the history of both countries; demographic analyses and information about current social, political, economic, educational, and religious institutions; and information about differences in learning styles, such as "field sensitive" and "field independent" learners (see Castenada, Ramirez, and Herold 1974).

The preservice workshops, particularly the cultural component, were an essential feature of the project for reasons that Smith (1987:18), if anything, understates: "Academic training never fully prepares the teacher for survival-level instruction." The typical ESL teacher today may have a master's degree and training in a program emphasizing linguistics and English structure, ESL curriculum and teaching methodologies, and an internship or other practical ESL experience. Generally, such training probably focuses upon highly literate adult learners with strong educational backgrounds and instrumental motivation (the typical university-based English-for-foreign-students center experience), or else upon "educable" non-adults (the conventional K-12 public school bilingual or ESL program). The differences between such conventional ESL training and the realities teachers must confront in programs aimed at adult refugees are vast.

Based upon our experience, several conclusions about ESL teacher training are warranted. First, it is apparent that a large number of future ESL jobs in the U.S. will be in programs aimed at adult refugees. Children of refugees, fortunately, have educational opportunities provided by public school systems, which in most communities are increasingly sensitive to their needs. Their parents and relatives are another matter. While recent influxes of Indo-Chinese, Cuban, and Haitian entrants have subsided somewhat, our experience of the past decade in dealing with such populations has been instructive. Nothing seems so inevitable as world political and economic tensions, and crises from the Caribbean and Central America to the Middle East may at any moment again make the U.S. a refuge for many. Our national experience over two centuries suggests that we will receive such refugees both to their, and our own, benefit and enrichment.

Second, in view of the above, greater attention must be given in ESL teacher training programs to models designed for refugee populations. Methodology courses must devote some attention to creating, evaluating, and using instructional materials designed for adults (especially those of limited education and literacy), and to instructional techniques appropriate for such learners.

More teacher training courses need to include cultural components that address not merely the usual observations about Japanese manners or Cuban proxemics, but also the psychological and cultural parameters and problems of pre-literates and those of limited educational backgrounds. Internship programs, where possible, might incorporate some experience in teaching and/or observing in refugee programs.

Finally, refugee programs themselves may increasingly adopt a bilingual vocational education model (such as those discussed by Galvan 1982, Friedenberg and Bradley 1983, and others), in which ESL training is actually integrated into, and inseparable from, the vocational or technical curriculum. Many ESL teachers of the future, therefore, may be staff members of vocational-technical institutions, not plying their craft *in vacuo*, but in "the shop," concerned with such things as safety language, operating manuals, the G.E.D., and the world of work. Such prospects strongly suggest the need for some exposure to the parameters of adult education and vocational and technical programs and settings in ESL training.

In the instructional program itself, our project staff found that time invested in the preservice workshops was amply repaid. The initial referrals, based upon BVOPT scores, were assigned to either Level 1 (199 or less on BVOPT), or Level 2 (200 or more on BVOPT). For the Level 1 groups, work in listening comprehension and foundations for beginning literacy in English proceeded rapidly, relying initially on audiovisual and other techniques, with written material incorporated as quickly as curricular consideration permitted. The Level 2 group, of course, was able to rely more heavily upon written materials.

The Thursday night home management sessions provided valuable information on an enormous variety of topics, beginning with the Center for Applied Linguistics' audiovisual *Your New Life in the United States* in Cuban Spanish and Haitian Creole. This introduced participants to essential aspects of everyday life, ranging from the use of flush toilets to hospital emergency rooms. Subsequent sessions focused upon such topics as social service agencies and organizations, religious institutions, grocery shopping, health and medical services and appointments, social security cards, contraception and family planning, and job interviews, with frequent visits by appropriate speakers whose presentations were assisted by the bilingual aides.

An important feature of our program was the integration of the home management and ESL components. The home management information became a large part of the content of the ESL instruction, and the home management presentations, though often requiring some translation back-up, nonetheless provided an increasing body of comprehensible input (see Krashen 1982, Krashen and Terrell 1983, and Krashen 1985). Language acquisition theory and research indicates that the process of acquiring a second language proceeds best when input is provided that is: (a) comprehensible, (b) relevant to the acquirer, (c) not grammatically sequenced, and (d) adequate in quantity. In this case, relevant input can be defined as both the form and content of messages that are useful for survival or the ability to function outside the classroom. The case against sequencing of structures in the research literature (e.g., Krashen 1982) is so persuasive that one is compelled to disagree with Smith (1987) and others supporting a survival-English syllabus based upon a sequence of grammatical structures that must be mastered through drill and repetition on a level by level basis.

Not only does a sequenced, lock-step structure syllabus fly in the face of the evidence supporting the "natural order hypothesis" (Krashen 1982), it is inimical to the goals of survival English programs where there is a premium upon rapid progress and a constraint upon time for achieving results. Smith (1987:24) claims that "it is important . . . to avoid the temptation to push students too quickly." Our experience suggests just the opposite: given the needs, students cannot be pushed fast enough. Our goal of advancing the students by one level (as measured by the BVOPT at exit) was accomplished for more than two-thirds of the students without formal attention to the requirements of grammatical sequencing. (The unsuccessful one-third was characterized by a high rate, 50% or more, of work-related absenteeism.)

Our experience did appear to support the claims of Long (1983; 1985) that the formal language instruction provided positively influenced the rate of acquisition, and possibly the ultimate level of ESL attainment. The progress of the students in nine weeks (as measured by the BVOPT) exceeded our most sanguine expectations, which were based upon norms in the literature.

The home management material not only provided a large part of the content of the ESL component, but also dictated many of the teaching strategies, techniques, and classroom activities. Many vocabulary items were drawn from the presentations. In addition, audiovisual aids such as pictures, hands-on demonstration items (tools with name labels, small appliances, etc.), music (current popular songs), and filmstrips were used extensively. Teachers also required participants to engage in an enormous amount of role-playing. Application forms of every conceivable kind (from Social Security to job applications) were duplicated for students to fill out and submit in simulated interview situations. Telephone extensions (with the teacher "offstage") were used for realistic practice in non-face-to-face conversational interaction. Mock medical appointments, shopping trips, and job interviews were regular features. In addition to these specialized activities, conventional teaching techniques and written material were used to increase student sophistication in test-taking and to lay the foundation for further education and training.

During these processes, certain cultural differences between the Haitians and Cubans became apparent. Cuban students were generally more loquacious, more sophisticated, and enthusiastic participants in the role-playing activities. Haitians, on the other hand, were generally more shy, reticent, and reluctant to do more than the minimum required in any individualized performance activity. The aversion the Haitians demonstrated toward drawing any undue attention to themselves can be interpreted in terms of both cultural preferences and socioeconomic and political conditions in Haiti. These differences were so marked that they became a source of resentment between the two groups. The Haitians seemed to regard the Cubans as boisterous, arrogant, ungrateful, and disrespectful toward teachers and administrators. Many of the Cubans seemed to regard the Haitians as stupid, uneducable, and unworthy of respect. This sort of ethnic stereotyping was not without its ironies. It soon became apparent that there were pronounced differences among the Cubans themselves in their attitudes toward the Haitians. Urbanized Cubans with educational attainments (regardless of how modest) tended to be the most intolerant; those with rural backgrounds, particularly from Oriente Province or other areas with a history of immigration by Haitians or other Caribbean Blacks, tended to be more tolerant and accepting of the Haitians. One benefit of the program, therefore, may have been a reduction of cultural and racial stereotyping in the attitudes of the participants as they studied and progressed together.

Overall, the target goal of receiving 150 referrals was met. Participants who completed the first nine-week Level 1 course were offered the opportunity to continue in Level 2 for an additional nine weeks, and most elected to do so. The practice was therefore continued in subsequent sessions. Counselors worked with those completing Level 2 to place them in vocational training or jobs. Ultimately, more than 80% of the students completed at least one level in the program. Both absenteeism and attrition fell well within predicted norms. This was a surprising finding, since the only inducement for participation offered students was free transportation to and from class. These findings thus dispute the conventional belief that immigrants with limited educational backgrounds and low socioeconomic status would be less motivated or educable than the immigrant population as a whole. To be sure, these participants represented the products of a winnowing process: they had risked immigration in the first place; they had moved from their ports of entry to Tampa; they had enrolled in the program; and they had persisted in it despite serious economic and personal obstacles.

Attrition and absenteeism, in the majority of cases, were not attributable to ineducability, lack of motivation, or frustration, but rather to employment factors. Most participants had, or were seeking, entry-level jobs (such as dishwasher, janitor, garbage collector, domestic, busboy, or agricultural laborer) in which English communication requirements were minimal; thus, they participated in the program because they correctly perceived that improvement in their economic opportunities would positively correlate with their command of English.

CONCLUSIONS

Some of the conclusions to be derived from our experience are evident in the foregoing discussion. To recapitulate, they are:

1. Traditional ESL assumptions, models, curricula, materials, and methodologies are inappropriate for and generally irrelevant to the needs of adult refugee populations with low levels of literacy and education.

2. Traditional ESL teacher training programs do not adequately prepare professionals to teach in programs aimed at such populations.

3. Despite severe psychological and educational handicaps, such populations appear to be as strongly motivated and potentially as educable as the LEP population in general.

4. The content of programs for such students is more important to progress than the structure of the syllabus.

Despite our measure of success, most (perhaps all) of the so-called survival-level ESL programs designed for refugees, including ours, are probably a waste of time for adult male entrants of impoverished educational backgrounds. This claim has nothing to do with the educability of this LEP population. Adult male refugees, regardless of educational background, are generally heads-of-households, and as such must of necessity seek and find employment in order to support their families as quickly as possible. Educational programs of any kind, therefore, are luxuries in the face of immediate needs. It is not surprising, therefore, that all adult males in our program were gainfully employed at least some of the time they were pursuing study. It is also not surprising that they were employed in entry-level jobs requiring a minimum of communication skills in English.

Because their work ethic is perhaps less atrophied, refugees constitute a significant national resource. Thus, providing them with opportunities for vocational training so they may better their standards of living is not simply humane treatment but positively in the national interest. The most significant cultural observation one can make about this particular LEP population is that intercultural differences within the various ethnic groups pale into insignificance beside their cultural commonalities. That is, socioeconomic status is itself a cultural parameter in which differences between the lows and the highs in educational background is greater than those between ethnic groups when socioeconomic background is not considered.

ESL has an indispensable role in the assimilation process, but for heads-of-households, ESL programs must be integrated with, rather than prior to, vocational education. The model I have in mind is, of course, the Galvan (1982) bilingual vocational educational model. The bilingual vocational ESL process is carried on in the vocational school, on the job, or both. Experience indicates that this process is much more effective in terms of cost, time expended, and ultimate level of achievement (both in ESL and vocational skills) than either pre-vocational or separate parallel (or pull-out) approaches of the type widely used (Friedenberg and Bradley 1981). In the final analysis, then, survival or pre-vocational ESL programs for heads-of-households can be justified only if they are extremely short-term in duration, and lead immediately into bilingual vocational education programs.

References

Castaneda, A., M. Ramirez, and P. Herold, 1974. *New Approaches to Bilingual, Bicultural Education.* Austin, TX: Dissemination Center for BE.

Friedenberg, J., and C. Bradley, 1981. *The Vocational ESL Handbook.* Rowley, MA: Newbury House.

Galvan, M., 1982. "Serving the LEP Population." Address to LEP Vocational Educators Workshop, Florida International University, Miami, FL.

Krashen, S., 1982. *Principles and Practice in Second Language Acquisition.* New York: Pergamon.

Krashen, S., 1985. *The Input Hypothesis.* New York: Longman.

Krashen, S., and T. Terrell, 1983. *The Natural Approach: Language Acquisition in the Classroom.* New York: Pergamon.

Long, M., 1983. "Does Second Language Instruction Make a Difference?" *TESOL Quarterly* 17, 3: 359–382.

Long, M., 1985. "Instructed Interlanguage Development." In *Issues in Second Language Acquisition,* edited by L. Beebe. Rowley, MA: Newbury House.

Lopez-Valadez, J., 1982. "Programs and Resources for Serving the LEP." Address to LEP Vocational Educators Workshop, Florida International University, Miami, FL.

Smith, S., 1987. "Teaching Survival-Level ESL." In *A TESOL Professional Anthology: Grammar and Composition,* edited by C. Cargill. Lincolnwood, IL: National Textbook Company.

Definitions of Bilingual-Bicultural Education

ANGELA LUPO-ANDERSON

D IFFICULTIES IN DEVELOPING a sound empirical base supportive of bilingual education are largely the result of a lack of a common definition and model for bilingual education and its relationship to English as a second language instruction. The variety of attempts to define bilingual education and English as a second language, as well as to describe an appropriate model, has resulted in misinterpretations of requirements for a quality program and consequential program implementation problems.

Problems of bilingual education implementation have created a struggle between those who formulate policy—administrators and legislators—and those who implement it—bilingual educators in the field. Professionals view the controversy as the need to determine whether bilingual education should be expanded, cut back, narrowed in focus, or broadened. Officials question whether bilingual education should remain a compensatory program which provides the transition for non- or limited English-speaking students to English monolingualism, or whether programs which foster true bilingualism should be developed instead.

Bilingual programs' problems have become complicated, involving other school issues, policies, economics, politics, and an entanglement which has caused bilingual education to be easily misunderstood. To correct the misconception that bilingual education should be implemented exclusively for any one ethnic group, Reynaldo Macias (1978) defined bilingual education as a strategy for teaching and reaching any population, not just Hispanics. Although bilingual education is not a panacea for all problems, it may be seen as a strategy which addresses the school's failure to provide adequate education for students of limited English-speaking ability.

Rudolph Troike echoed the quandary in his statement which attributed U.S. Congressmen's apathy toward bilingual education to a failure to understand what is involved. Robert Di Pietro based his similar conviction on a study of Congress (1977) which he conducted with the assistance of graduate researchers. Di Pietro found that most legislators could not give a definition of either "bilingualism" or "bilingual education," although they had appropriated millions of dollars to bilingual projects over the last nine years.

Perhaps conflicting definitions and models of bilingual education have frustrated legislators' attempts to understand it; professionals in the field have experienced similar circumvention.

In its first annual mandated report to the President and Congress in June 1975, the National Advisory Council on Bilingual Education (established by the 1974 amendment to the Bilingual Education Act of 1968) defined bilingual education as:

> a process in which English and other languages and cultures that reflect the makeup of the community are used in instruction. It is designed to meet the unique language and culture needs of each student, regardless of origin.

The U.S. Commission of Education described bilingual education as a transitional process in a publication upon which many school officials have based their interpretations:

> Bilingual bicultural education is a comprehensive educational approach which involves more than just imparting English skills. Children are taught all cognitive areas, first in their native language. Oral expression and reading are developed in native language courses, and English is taught formally in English as a second language classes. Once the children have learned to speak English, they are taught to read it. Instruction in areas which do not require extensive use of language such as art, music, and physical education may be provided in English for informal language practice and exposure. Instruction through English in cognitive areas begins when the child can function in that language and experiences no academic handicap due to insufficient knowledge of the language. Some instruction in the

native language may continue even after the child is competent in English.

Andersson and Boyer (1970) stress the importance of developing a bicultural curriculum for the benefit of dominant English-speakers as well as for limited English-speakers by integrating the cultural aspects of the non-English language into the dominant English-language arts curriculum.

Non-English-dominant students whose dominant language is used for wider communication should be prepared to read in that language. Because the techniques for teaching reading readiness vary according to languages, the school should consult with native reading teachers of the language in developing the language arts curriculum. In the absence of existing models for instruction in local languages, Andersson and Boyer (1970) propose the following objectives for a language arts curriculum in a local language:

1. Introduce reading to students in the language they know best; and

2. Encourage familiarity with the indigenous language and its literature—written and oral; encourage further literacy production.

Andersson and Boyer (1970) believe that ESL is a vital part of the language arts curriculum for non-English-speaking students learning English. They contend that literacy in English should follow speaking and understanding. Bicultural content is essential to render language arts materials meaningful.

Foreign language instructional methodology may be adapted in a language arts curriculum for dominant English-speakers learning the minority language. However, it is important to acknowledge that the non-English language is not "foreign," but a legitimate language spoken by members of the community.

The social studies component is a principal vehicle for presenting the bicultural aspects of the curriculum. Andersson and Boyer (1970) suggest that diversity among people and their cultures should be accorded better status in the curriculum.

Because the scientific and mathematical disciplines are rapidly becoming international in content, no one language or culture should monopolize the potential for breakthroughs in these areas. Selection of the appropriate language for content area instruction must be determined to a great extent by the quality and availability of materials written in the target language.

The art and music component of the curriculum could be best utilized to develop multicultural appreciation. Cultural differences should also be integrated into the health and physical education components in order to avoid imposition of American standards on students who possess different values and viewpoints. Andersson and Boyer (1970) indicate that the use of role-playing and kinesics in the health and physical education components can promote cross-cultural understanding as well as educate students for a healthy life.

Andersson and Boyer (1970) base their discussion of the time distribution for language use in each subject on Mackey's typology of curriculum patterns. They state that the goal of an effectively designed bilingual curriculum should be to achieve equal distribution of languages for instruction.

Typically, the students' dominant language should be used as the instructional language while they are learning English. As students acquire English language proficiency, the percentage of time devoted to native (dominant) language instruction decreases as English language instruction increases, until both languages achieve equal time distribution for subject matter. The same language distribution treatment applies in two-way bilingual education programs in which dominant English speakers are learning the minority language.

In selecting the most appropriate methods and materials for a curriculum design, Andersson and Boyer (1970) consider three ideas essential for incorporating the necessary elements of a bilingual-bicultural curriculum: splitting the time assigned for instruction in a subject between the two languages; teaching some subjects in one language, some in the other language; and combining time-splitting and subject allotment for various approaches.

An assessment of available materials should precede any selection or development of materials. Andersson and Boyer (1970) warn that assessment of available resources is especially critical for teachers and administrators new to the field because they may erroneously conclude that no materials are available or suitable for their bilingual education needs. Materials should be reviewed according to their potential suitability for the age and interest level, range of difficulty, subject area, culture or subculture, and linguistic group represented by each student. In the absence of suitable materials, materials may be created.

Andersson and Boyer's (1970) schema of instructional staffing patterns uses paraprofessionals as well as certified teachers. The teacher aide provides a link between the monolingual student and teacher when neither speak the same language.

Monolingual English-speaking teachers should be sympathetic toward the limited English-speaking students and understanding of bilingual schooling. Furthermore, Andersson and Boyer (1970) believe that monolingual English-speaking teachers should not teach any subjects in English to limited English-speaking students unless the teachers have been trained specifically in ESL techniques.

Ideally, Andersson and Boyer (1970) feel that each teacher in the bilingual program should be proficient in both languages and should be assigned to a self-contained classroom. Although the bilingual teacher in a self-contained classroom may have many advantages, using two or more than two teachers in a team-teaching approach is preferred. Teachers can then concentrate on their subject matter strengths in the language they know best. The team-teaching approach contributes authenticity to the students' language development and quality to their cognitive development.

Because no requirements for teacher certification existed specifically for bilingual education at the time of Andersson and Boyer's publication, the authors refer to the Modern Language Association's "Qualifications of Teachers of Foreign Languages" which could be modified for bilingual education purposes and measured by the MLA's Foreign Language Proficiency Tests. Andersson and Boyer (1970) suggest that teacher candidates for bilingual program placement submit their scores on the proficiency tests as evidence of language ability. Recruitment and selection of teachers will probably necessitate extensive preservice and inservice preparation, since bilingual teacher education programs are not numerous. Because it is essential that the bilingual program teacher of the non-dominant language must speak and understand the dialectal variations of the limited English-speaking students, it will often be necessary to transform unprepared native speakers into bilingual teachers.

A related alternative for staffing is the recruitment of native language teachers in foreign countries. Adequate orientation to the American culture, educational system, and the particular setting must be given considerable attention in order to avoid the debilitating effects of culture shock and displacement.

Evaluation is the final component which Andersson and Boyer (1970) include in their curriculum planning guidelines. The three areas which should be reviewed to determine program quality are teacher qualifications, the children's learning, and the overall effectiveness of the bilingual program. An update of language scores for the non-dominant language will provide one important indicator of teacher qualifications. Diagnostic tests administered in each language at the beginning of each year will provide a measure of the students' language proficiency. An annual assessment of students' academic achievement in content and skill areas for both languages should be compared with the students' scores from the previous year to determine the bilingual program's effectiveness. In addition, Andersson and Boyer (1970) suggest that program effectiveness be assessed in terms of planning and administration, community support, school board performance, school administration, teachers, parents, students, testing, teachers' and principals' evaluations, and a comparison of program outcomes with objectives.

Saville-Troike's bilingual education model reflects Andersson and Boyer's thinking regarding instructional staffing and her strong professional background in linguistics and ESL. Saville-Troike stipulates that, ideally, the teacher in the bilingual program should be qualified to provide both native language instruction (NLI) and ESL. An acceptable alternative is a team-teaching approach, in which each teacher uses a different language of instruction. Each teacher should have knowledge of the other language, although native language instruction will be delivered in the teacher's dominant language. The NLI teacher provides instruction in content areas, skill development (language arts) and translates as needed to ensure that learning in the second language is meaningful. The ESL teacher provides ESL as well as English content instruction. Saville-Troike claims that all instruction in English is ESL when English is the learner's second language. This approach requires close cooperation between the teachers in a unit to plan complementary learning activities.

Saville-Troike rejects the staffing combination utilizing a monolingual English-speaking teacher with a bilingual aide because the monolingual English-speaking teacher lacks the linguistic competence to develop the students' native language, an essential component of bilingual education. Moreover, the monolingual teacher of English provides a negative role model for non-English-speaking students.

Saville-Troike considers the critical decision in bilingual education curriculum development to be what content to provide in which language. The availability of content area materials in the target language is the major determining factor.

Some subjects should be taught exclusively in one language to eliminate language interference. Repeating instruction in both languages ignores the transferability of concepts across languages. Saville-Troike's suggestions regarding provision of science and math instruction differ from Andersson and Boyer's. Because sciences are taught typically in English in the U.S., Saville-Troike claims that it is better to teach this subject matter in English as early as possible to develop the necessary specialized vocabulary.

The "Cardenas-Cardenas Theory of Incompatibility" states that the instructional needs of minority language students are incompatible with the instruction offered in the schools because public school instruction is designed for Anglo-Saxon, white, middle-class students.

Cardenas contends that the instructional program should be designed according to the learners' characteristics in order to reverse their pattern of academic failure. Cardenas' theory identifies poverty, culture, language, mobility, and societal perceptions as the major categorical incompatibilities in typical curricula.

Child development in poverty-level situations is not the same as child development in middle-class home environments. Child/adult ratios, which are usually large in lower-income areas, contribute to abnormal speech development due to a lack of adequate adult interactions with children. The absence of communication media, success models, and intellectually stimulating activities, combined with the effects of poor housing, malnutrition, and poor health influence the development of poor children.

Although an educational handicap may develop as a result of poverty and related circumstances, Cardenas professes that the handicap is not serious if the instructional program compensates for a learner's deficient entry-level competencies. A real handicap develops when the child is placed in an educational program which disregards the learner's entering characteristics, considering only the developmental patterns of middle-class children.

Incompatibilities between the cultural characteristics of minority children and typical instructional programs are summarized below:

1. Most school personnel know nothing about the cultural characteristics of the school's minority population.

2. The few school personnel who are aware of these cultural characteristics seldom do anything about them.

3. On those rare occasions when the school does attempt to do something about the culture of minority groups, it always does the wrong thing.

Cardenas cites studies by Lessor and Kagan and Madsen which support the premise that a child's learning capacity is a function of his or her ethnicity, race, related cultural characteristics, culturally preferred learning styles, and those preferred by the school. Cardenas distinguishes between the effects of culture and the effects of poverty. The school district's responsibility is to eradicate the effects of poverty, not culture. Culturally different children are deprived when institutions act to remove all semblances of their native culture.

Language incompatibilities develop when the language of instruction is different from that of the child. Children must be taught in a language they understand. Cardenas believes that ESL and immersion programs alone are inappropriate to resolve language incompatibilities; bilingual education is the only solution. Cognitive development in both languages as well as development of the native and second languages are vital components of Cardenas' plan. Second language development is provided by ESL, one of the three essential areas of his model.

Instructional incompatibilities related to student mobility pose unique challenges to the school district. The traditional curriculum, which was designed for highly stable children, assumes that the children will learn as a result of curriculum continuity and sequence. The highly mobile child, either the agricultural migrant or the urban minority child, forfeits these benefits.

Incompatibilities in the societal perceptions of minority children also render the typical instructional program inadequate. Minority children perceive themselves negatively, whereas most instructional programs have been designed for students with positive self-concept. The curriculum assumes that minority students have previously developed cognitive and affective prerequisite skills, neglecting necessary reinforcement through an absence of adequate materials and techniques. It is believed that children will achieve success if given the opportunity, since success is motivated by prior successful experiences. Similarly, citing the work of Jacobson and Rosenthal in developing the theory of the "Pygmalion effect," minority students generally comply with the schools' low performance expectancies.

Cardenas counsels that any resolution of the five variables affecting curricular incompatibilities should recognize that the variables are interrelated and interdependent. The negative effects of incompatibilities between the instructional program and learner needs should be counteracted by a comprehensive plan which considers the interaction of the five variables.

Schools must adapt the curriculum to the individual learner's needs, rather than the learner having to adapt to the school's instructional program. Cardenas advises that past instructional methods and expectations have been discriminatory. A person's linguistic/cultural orientation cannot be totally transformed; not even legislation prohibiting instruction in a language other than English has stopped it. Although ideas of cultural pluralism are gradually replacing the "melting pot" theory, changing the individual to meet the characteristics of the instructional program will not succeed as long as society discriminates socially, politically, economically, and militarily against Mexican-American, Black American, and other minority students. Expecting Mexican-Americans, Blacks, and others to assume an entirely new identity is a destructive method of change.

The major goal of bilingual/bicultural education is to provide the learner with an equal chance for success in education. This can be accomplished by the twofold effect of providing language and content instruction in the child's dominant and second language in math, reading, social studies, and science. Inherent in this process is the child's demonstrated success in reading his or her native language before second language reading instruction is introduced.

ESL in bilingual education provides the learner with skills to function in an English-dominant society. Like instruction in traditional audiolingual classes, ESL in bilingual education is intensively language-oriented; but in addition, students are given the opportunity to combine second language and content area learning in a structured, sequential manner. Meaningful learning in various content areas is more feasible because of the child's initial introduction to the content material in the dominant language.

Therefore, the ESL role in bilingual education is not to remove the "language handicap" in non-English speakers. It is viewed as a means for providing the student with the necessary content and skills for success in the second language. Although the intent is to equip the learner with survival skills in the dominant culture, it is not intended to be a transitional medium. Bilingual/bicultural education with a clearly defined and developed ESL component gives students an opportunity to move *across* languages and cultures, thereby providing them with optimum chances for self-actualization.

REFERENCES

Andersson, Theodore, and Mildred Boyer, 1970. *Bilingual Schooling in the United States,* 2 vols. Austin, TX: Southwest Educational Development Laboratory I, p. 12.

Cardenas, 1974. "An Educational Plan for the Denver Public Schools." National Educational Task Force de la Raza, San Antonio, TX. January 21, (excerpts), in *Bilingual-Bicultural Education: A Handbook for Attorneys and Community Workers.* Cambridge, MA: Center for Law and Education.

Center for Law and Education, 1985. *Bilingual-Bicultural Education: A Handbook for Attorneys and Community Workers.* Cambridge, MA.

Finocchiaro, Mary, 1969. *Teaching English as a Second Language.* New York: Harper and Row.

Hines, Mary Elizabeth, 1976. "A Critique of the U.S. Commission on Civil Rights Report on Bilingual-Bicultural Education." In *English as a Second Language in Bilingual Education: Selected TESOL Papers,* edited by James E. Alatis and Kristie Twaddell; 21–33. Washington, D.C.: Teachers of English to Speakers of Other Languages.

Macias, Reynaldo F., 1978. "The Bilingual Debate." *Nuestro: The Magazine for Latinos,* Feb.: 36.

National Advisory Council on Bilingual Education. *Bilingual Education: Quality Education for all Children* (Annual Report). Washington, D.C. (ED 117 964).

Saville, Muriel R., and Rudolph C. Troike, 1971. *A Handbook of Bilingual Education.* Washington, D.C.: Teachers of English to Speakers of Other Languages.

Saville-Troike, Muriel. "The Role of ESL in Bilingual Education." *Foundations for Teaching English as a Second Language: Theory and Method for Multicultural Education,* p. 133.

U.S. Commission on Civil Rights. *A Better Chance to Learn: Bilingual–Bicultural Education,* p. 29.

U.S. Congress, Senate, Committee on Labor and Public Welfare, Education Legislation, 1973. *Hearings Before a Subcommittee on Education of the Senate Committee on Labor and Public Welfare on S. 1539,* 93rd Congress, 1st session, p. 2600.

U.S. Department of Health, Education and Welfare, Office of Education, 1970. *Manual for Project Applicants and Grantees: Programs Under Bilingual Education Act.* Title VII, ESEA-Draft, March 30: 1.

Multicultural Education

DAN MCCAULEY

WHAT ARE SOME of the important assumptions surrounding multicultural education these days? Are they relevant to today's educational scene? That depends on the plot and the setting, as well as on the characters or ethnic groups who will take part in the scene.

People want control over their own destinies, over their own lives, and over the institutions which shape their lives. If they do not have control over their institutions, the economic system, the police, the military, the schools, etc., they are placed in the position of being victims who are powerless, impotent, and dehumanized. They may either react by igniting in anger or by becoming underground revolutionaries as Oscar Acosta once threatened to do in the early '70s in Gomez's (1971) article, "Chicanos: Strangers in Their Own Land."

At another end of this same spectrum is Freire's (1970), "Culture of Silence," which is infused with the concept of "will of God" (p. 10). This fatalistic assumption conceives of a world in which one can do nothing; people are powerless, and their only choice is to accept the situation and bear it in silence. This concept is also prevalent in the "macho" tradition which, in many senses, victimizes Chicano, Mexican, and South American women. *Five Mexican American Women in Transition* (Lindborg and Ovondo 1977: 19) states that the wife "must never express sorrow or anger at her husband's extramarital activities" because her role is one of silent suffering. This should be viewed, however, as a transitory situation, since many Mexican-American women are becoming more vocal.

Consequently, inherent in both these assumptions (the one violent, the other silent) is the sense of desperation and lack of choice which minorities have. The literature often seems to suggest that we can give them a third choice—the school. What society cannot solve may, in some way, be better dealt with through the multicultural school. Valverde (1978) once advanced his "Strategies for the Advancement of Cultural Pluralism"; Harold G. Shane (1973), his futuristic "Reassessment of Educational Issues of the 1970s"; Hector Farias (1971), his "Mexican-American Values and Attitudes Toward Education"; and Ovondo (1977), his "School Implications of the Peaceful Latino Invasion."

But can the schools meet these expectations and maintain the cultural boundaries of these various groups? One wonders, because as Gordon (1964) noted in his book, *Assimilation in American Life,* "Once structural assimilation has occurred, either simultaneously with or subsequent to acculturation, all the other types of assimilation will naturally follow" (p. 81). This implies that once people gain admittance to various economic, social, and cultural institutions, they begin to identify with these institutions. Such members of the minority population will no longer feel victimized by those institutions, just as the white middle and upper classes do not. They will simply have joined the power structure, have a stronger sense of control in their lives, and end up identifying and supporting the institutions that their fathers hated.

Can the schools be used to maintain an ethnic group's cultural boundaries? When members of a minority group join other institutions which are not multicultural, can their ethnic identity and culture really be preserved? Is it possible that we may simply end up with third and fourth generation Anglos who can speak Spanish? The school is only one institution, and expecting it to act alone may be asking too much.

Multicultural education may only be with us as long as we have groups who are either not white or who have just arrived in the U.S. Perhaps boundaries can only be kept in a theistic sense, such as the Jewish people have done. Judaism is a religion—Chicanoism is not. Black is a skin color—brown is very close to white. There are many families on Guam whose daughters and sons have married white Anglo-Saxons. Perhaps this is what has happened to many Orientals, to some native Americans, and to many Latinos. Does it really make any difference? If people's differences are not a matter of right and wrong, or good, better, and best, could it be said that "different" is simply to maintain cultural choice? What choice did we all have originally when we were born into our own cultures?

Is the purpose of education simply to maintain that choice multiculturally, or ultimately to teach us to cope with the reality of change? Perhaps, as some of the literature suggests (e.g., Ovondo 1977, Valverde 1978, and Shane 1973), the answer is to be found in both culture and change: Culture—the land of my ancestors, and Coping—the land of my change.

DILEMMAS OF MULTICULTURAL EDUCATION

Why is there so much ferment in multicultural education? Probably because there is so much boiling, popping, and stewing in the ingredients that go into it. Thus, any discussion of this pot of dilemmas should look not only at linguistic and basic sociocultural assumptions, but also at philosophy and history.

Philosophically, there is ferment in multicultural education because it lends itself to the dilemma posed by cultural relativism. The essence of cultural relativism, according to G. F. Kneller (1965), is that "Every culture is unique and therefore must be analyzed on its own terms . . . The virtue of the cultural relativist is that he eschews ethnocentrism" (pp. 31–32). However, there is a trap in this thinking which limits conceptualization beyond a certain point. Kneller says that "cultural relativism is a form of moral relativism for it implies that moral values are valid only for the culture that holds them. It implies, for example, that we have no right to condemn apparent cruelties in the customs of other peoples, because to do so is to extend our own values beyond the only context in which they are legitimate. The great merit of this kind of moral relativism is that it makes us tolerant of other cultures and unwilling to settle their affairs in the name of our own values . . . The cultural relativist also implies that only individuals can be maladjusted, not culture . . . Also, relativism makes it impossible to improve our own culture by adopting other cultures' values that we might believe to be superior because relativism makes it nonsensical to regard such values as superior to all" (pp. 32–34).

On the other side are the cultural universalists. Their contention is, according to Kneller, that "in important respects, the human lot is universal . . . All cultures must come to terms with the universal necessities of human living . . . All cultures set moral limits to violence, maintain a sense of loyalty, have certain ways of winning a livelihood, have codified family systems, a language, etc." (pp. 37–38). This, of course, implies moral universalism, which "when carried to extreme maintains that whether or not man observes it, an objective moral order is enjoined on him as a rational being" (Bidney 1962: 446). The trap here is that "the universalist may distort the particular facts of different cultures in order to fit them into his all too comprehensive categories. The other is that he runs the risk of applying the norms of his own culture to the human race as a whole" (Kneller 1965: 41).

The second basic dilemma which stems from this philosophical conflict concerns basic linguistic assumptions. These are obviously inherent in articles such as Brazil's (1980) "The Political Mayhem Over Bilingual Education." On one side you have educators who feel that English should be the medium of instruction because, as the standard language of American culture, it is the best language to learn. These educators are afraid that if children are not taught English, they will maintain their primary language and culture rather than master English. Such educators contend this will just lead California, for example, into becoming another Quebec. On the other side of the issue stand the bilingual educators who maintain that, after all, children learn best in the language they know best.

Contiguous to this position are the politicians who must vote on the states' school budget for bilingual education, which often represents many millions of dollars. Of course, in many states they will have the strong tendency to represent their constituents' assumptions, beliefs, and values. Thus, in some cases, Anglos, Chicanos, and politicians from other cultures may often seem to see things in the emotional light of ethnocentrism. This adds to the political ferment. In the final analysis, bilingualism should be seen as viable in the sense that both languages have different purposes and uses to the individual.

The third area of ferment is caused by the basic sociocultural assumptions under which cultures in the political arena are operating. Since stereotyping is perhaps the most dominant theme here, it must be looked at as the most serious problem confronting the bilingual educator. Ethnic minorities and majorities both form these stereotypes within our society, often in a haphazard fashion. Sometimes, as Banks (1979) suggests, children are encapsulated with stereotypes before even having a chance to develop an alternate view. Teachers are not immune to this. Consequently, they may unconsciously stereotype a particular group as belonging to a certain economic level, or as being in certain trades or professions.

Longstreet (1978) seems to feel, however, that stereotyping is at the heart of an ethnic study. She justifies her assertion under the premise that scientific processes, while limited in what they attempt, are perhaps the best methods of approaching and debunking false stereotypes based on prejudice, lack of information, and gossip. She then qualifies this statement by being sure the format of her methodology is approached through the definitional concept of "ongoing tentativeness" (p. 13).

Perhaps Longstreet is right. Is it possible that one can never get away from this idea? Teachers in a school which has a multicultural environment must know certain cultural traits that are based on scientific study rather than on gossip. They need to recognize, for example, that Chicanos may walk a certain way or that Blacks may roll their eyes when they talk. If they don't, then these kinds of perceptions may cause problems and additional ferment which will affect their teaching.

A certain amount of ferment accompanies almost any new immigrant group that comes to America. Such ferment can perhaps be understood if, as Banks (1979) suggests, we look at a group's ethnic history through their eyes. Oppression, loss of identity, acculturation, borrowing, and feelings of inferiority, coupled with feelings of not having received justice from American society, are common themes that some immigrants have left behind, while others still bitterly feel.

Thus, at the heart of the sociocultural and linguistic assumptions of various groups lies cultural conflict—whose only resolution may eventually rely on individual interaction, accommodation, and hopefully, understanding. However, as long as both groups maintain their strong identities, conflict is bound to occur as part of the processes of human interaction. Let's hope the ferment is as much wine as it is vinegar. Let us also remember that it is not only what you believe that provides a difference in taste, but how you use your beliefs that counts.

REFERENCES

Banks, J. A., 1979. *Teaching Strategies for Ethnic Studies.* 2nd ed. Boston: Allyn and Bacon, Inc.

Bidney, D., 1962. "The Concept of Value in Modern Anthropology." In *Anthropology Today,* edited by Sol Tax. Chicago: University of Chicago Press (Phoenix Books).

Brazil, E., 1980. "The Political Mayhem over Bilingual Education." *California Journal.* December: 435–437.

Farias, H., 1971. "Mexican American Values and Attitudes Toward Education." *Phi Delta Kappan* 52: 602–604.

Freire, P., 1970. *Pedagogy of the Oppressed.* New York: The Seabury Press.

Gomez, D., 1971. "Chicanos: Strangers in Their Own Land." *America* 124: 649–652.

Gordon, M. G., 1964. *Assimilation in American Life.* New York: Oxford University Press.

Kneller, G. F., 1965. *Educational Anthropology.* New York: John Wiley and Sons, Inc.

Lindborg, K., and E. J. Ovando, 1977. *Five Mexican American Women in Transition: A Case Study of Migrants in the Midwest.* San Francisco: R & E Research Associates, Inc.

Longstreet, W. S., 1978. *Aspects of Ethnicity.* New York and London: Teachers College Press.

Ovando, C. J., 1977. "School Implications of the Peaceful Latino Invasion." *Phi Delta Kappan* 59: 230–234.

Shane, H. G., 1973. "Looking to the future: Reassessment of Educational Issues of the 1970's." *Phi Delta Kappan* 54: 326–337.

Valverde, L. A., 1978. "Strategies for the Advancement of Cultural Pluralism." *Phi Delta Kappan* 60: 107–110.

Some Aspects of Saudi Culture

ERNEST FRECHETTE

O NE OF THE IMPORTANT TASKS for a language teacher is to prepare
students to communicate and understand people from other
parts of the world as well as people within their native language and
cultural community. Students must also be aware that there are universals as well as cultural differences among peoples. An extension of
this task is to relate what is taught in the classroom with the real
world, all the while making sure that students avoid stereotyping.

Among the several writers who have attempted to identify universals of culture are Nostrand (1978), who came up with his "Emergent
Model," a structured inventory of the main themes of a culture;
Murdock et al. (1964), with their Outline of Cultural Materials, an
anthropological inventory of behavior; and Cowan (1978), with his
universals: (a) material cultural, (b) the arts, play, and recreation,
(c) language and nonverbal communication, (d) social organizations,
(e) social control, (f) conflict and warfare, (g) economic organization,
(h) education, and (i) world view (p. 8).

This chapter will incorporate some of the universals found in Arab
culture as seen through the Saudi world view, religion, social life,
world of work, and education. Some comparisons will be made with
the U.S. culture. Our objective will be to show that there are some
common abilities, that one must respect differences, and that peoples'
beliefs, attitudes, and behaviors are shaped by their culture.

What is culture? Brooks (1968) defines it as follows: "Culture (relating to patterns of living) refers to the individual's role in the unending kaleidoscope of life situations of every kind and the rules and models for attitude and conduct in them. By reference to these models, every human being, from infancy onward, justifies the world to himself as best he can, associates with those around him, and relates to the social order to which he is attached" (p. 210). He further adds, "What is important in culture (defined above) is what one is expected to think, believe, say, do, eat, wear, pay, endure, resent, honor, laugh at, fight for, and worship, in typical like situations . . ." (p. 211).

Here are some predominant characteristics which can be helpful in understanding Arabs. In general, according to Althen (1978), one finds: (a) a tendency to seek leisure and to resign oneself; (b) a regard for the individual over institutions; (c) an imagery in thought and speech; (d) a highly hospitable people; (e) lovers of holidays and festivals; (f) a keen sense of beauty; and (g) self-esteem (pp. 115–116). Love and peace are reflected in their art and they are "less captivated by the distinctions between fact and fiction than by mystery, romance, poetry, imagination . . ." (Lacey 1981: 47).

THE ROLE OF RELIGION

The Islamic religion controls the general life style at all levels and prescribes the following five duties for all: faith (*shedadah*), prayer five times a day (*salat*), alms-giving (*zakat*), fasting during the Ramadan (*sawm*), and a pilgrimage to Mecca (*Hajj*).

Islam is totalitarian in nature, but there are signs that there have been some moves in Saudi Arabia to reduce the degree of control it has over mundane affairs: the slow decrease in power of the conservatives, a number of outsiders now in high places, the spread of central government, more use of Western ways, increasing opposition to the religious leaders (*ulema*), and control on daily life. In addition, slaves were freed in 1962, and tribal power and warfare have been either curbed or ended (Thompson and Reischauer 1966: 123).

One should be aware that at the beginning of the present long rule, Ibn Saud (the first king) and Mohammad al-Wahhab (preacher of Wahhabism, the strictest interpretation of the Koran) worked out an arrangement in which both were to defend and propagate Islam's Unitarian doctrine. The king's mandate is to obey the Lord, and consequently, religion and government work together. Here are some examples of the religion's influence on Saudi thinking and behavior: (a) God does not expect man to do what is not humanly possible;

(b) subscription to the principle of "an eye for an eye and a tooth for a tooth"; (c) the notions of forgiveness and turning the other cheek are unrealistically demanding; (d) the maximum number of wives is set at four, and man must treat his wives equitably; (e) punishment by death to adulterers using stoning, burning, or strangulation; (f) the outlawing of pork and its products; and (g) man is given a more dominant role (Sefein 1981: 162).

SOCIAL RELATIONS

One notes historical continuity and stability in the Saudi social model, as opposed to the frequent changes in our society. There is constant pressure to conform; people are shamed into conforming. Peer acceptance is of prime import.

To get along with all people is most important; Saudis do not like to offend strangers or have face-to-face confrontations with them. If you are a guest, they try to tell you what you want to hear. Gossip in public and public criticism are not considered dignified or acceptable.

For the Saudis, social relations are based on Islam, whose laws affect both the social and spiritual aspects of life. It is up to the government to see that the people can practice their faith and that the laws are adhered to. They are tolerant of others' beliefs and practices.

When talking, Arabs stand close, eye-to-eye; closeness is important. Touching, sharing, and pushing in public are natural, while at the same time, it is expected that everyone be treated with dignity and respect. Saying no to a request is considered impolite, but ways can be found to defer any action on the request; Saudis would rather be positively committal in refusing.

There are some absolute caveats: touching or giving something with the left hand, raising one's feet on a chair or desk, showing the soles of the feet, and drinking of alcohol (except in Egypt, Bahrain, and Lebanon).

The extended family, though showing some signs of weakening due to changing economy and growth in city living, is still strong. The family is larger than our own, patriarchal, and authoritarian. Practically all decisions are made by the male head, sometimes including the family, in job selection, marriage, school selection, and financial matters.

Lee (1980) states that "all social relationships are indirectly, if not directly, tied to family considerations . . . [that the family] is the strongest unifying force next to Islam itself" (pp. 13–14). She notes that the multiple-wife household is on its way out, and that family honor and its defense are still very strong. One's family is an index of how a person is judged. On the whole, Saudis are socially more conservative then Americans.

We encourage our youngsters' emancipation rather early, urging them to be on their own and to earn their way. This is quite foreign to the Arab culture, in which the family gives far greater support and relatives, friends, and neighbors are near. We like privacy; they like to be together in large houses. Thus, our single-family homes are not their cup of tea. They like to sit around and talk, especially in cafés as in Europe; our life is more individualistic and filled with varied activities.

Saudis prefer dealing with people on a personal basis, especially in business; it is also a way of getting things done or getting a job to go to someone who might be able to do something for them—they call it *intisab*. In the U.S., people are expected to go on their own merit.

Being accustomed to a less-defined sense of time, it is difficult for Saudis to look at specific time commitments. For them, "tomorrow" may mean "at a convenient time for them"; it is not a definitive word. They also often use expressions which delay an action because it is not important or urgent to them; "God willing" is a common expression for being noncommital or for explaining delay.

THE WORLD OF WORK

Work is a way of living, and all types of work are respected except gambling and prostitution. Islam is a strong advocate of work and respecter of knowledge. Those with money should enjoy it, but they should help those in need; it is illegal to lend money with interest. Begging, trying to impress with wealth, wasting money or food, and self-gratification are all frowned upon.

Public servants are respected, and they are expected to serve their own interests—however harmful they may be to the public. They regard nepotism as a social duty. "To the Westerner, alarming government inteference is often visible in the forms of (1) *de facto* administrative centralization (sometimes in direct contradiction to the established 'decentralized' machinery) and (2) the growth of miring bureaucracy. Saturated employment statistics and over-specialization are compounded by a severe envision of responsibility which is reflected in the inability to handle problems, a mania for interpreting rules and regulations down to the letter, and the incessant passing of the buck. Having personal contacts may or may not be helpful in short-cutting the bureaucratic plexus" (Bagnole 1976: 29).

It is almost certain that such behavior and traditional attitudes will hamper Saudi socioeconomic development; there appears to be a lack of enthusiasm and ability for innovation, perhaps due to their not seeing the necessity because of the new wealth. The changes that have taken place in the social environment during the 1970s have been rather insignificant in comparison with the economic shifts.

The family and the immediate loyalty due have a strong influence on an individual's behavior; this aspect tends to be translated to the administrative system. "Every individual in the family is primarily responsible for the well-being of his family; hence, he behaves according to the norms of his family and his behavior is determined by the family's patterns" (Alnimir 1981: 39). In spite of the tight grip of traditional structure, the change from the extended to the nuclear family is having a gradual eroding effect on the influence of the family; education has also been giving a helping hand in this matter.

Being selective in the type of work they do and looking down on manual labor, the bedouin family's negative attitude toward work "is not merely for economic incentives, but for societal satisfaction" (Alnimir 1981: 40). Saudi youth in academic and vocational schools, and illiterates (a) are "opposed to performing manual labor, (b) prefer government over private sector jobs, (c) prefer to work in urban rather than a rural area, and (e) consider job prestige more important than economic incentives" (Alnimir 1981: 35).

EDUCATION

Secondary and higher education surpassed the primary education growth rate in all Arab states during the 1970s. Notable trends include the extension of compulsory schooling, the reorganization and restructuring of secondary education to meet economic and social development, the promotion of scientific subjects for study, the growing number of females in secondary education, and the increase in the number of institutions of higher education.

Arab students who come to the U.S. are generally of the upper class, have a broad background in travel and languages, and often have had fine individual preparation in high-priced, private schools. They are frequently unhappy with many facets of our culture and the university life and its processes. This can well be attributed to their background, in which the family is a close unit and the society is traditional and authoritarian. They suffer from homesickness but they see education as a passport to a job or career, especially in the bureaucratic ladder.

Saudis do not regard cheating and copying as negatively as we do; if it is to help them achieve their goal or to help a friend, then they just do it; it may be a cultural influence. This is consonant "with the Islamic concept of 'darura'—necessity: if you are starving in the desert, then it is permissible to eat pork" (Lacey 1981: 475). Their educational background is very traditional, and most assignments involve memorization. They are often weak at taking tests.

Bagnole (1976) states that "If students' perception of Western style education is often distorted and marked by chronic absenteeism, chronic unpreparedness and absence of good study habits, apathy, and inadaptability even at the university level, the situation is further exacerbated by government interference, both deliberate and unconscious" (p. 26).

THE ROLE OF WOMEN

Islam has helped women by "limiting the number of wives a man might have, imposing restrictions on divorce, and insuring the rights of women to property and a share in the inheritance from father or husband" (Lee 1982: 16). However the male is still dominant. In marriage, the husband is master; divorce is his privilege. Marriage is contractual, and sex is to be consummated only in marriage. To have children is the main reason for marriage; birth control is not normally condoned, but contraception and termination are permitted to save a mother.

Modest dress is *de rigueur,* and so are the restraints on male-female relationships. Women are to be respected, but there are few in the business world. However, due to education, more are found in education and government ministries. If there is to be a change, it will most likely be a slow process, since the religious laws and the cultural heritage are so deeply entrenched.

Tradition says that "women's social activities outside the family should be segregated . . . But this did not prevent—rather, it encouraged—the formation of women's cooperative groups, and these women's collectives are today among the most active private associations in Saudi life" (Lacey 1981: 368).

To us the black veil is stereoptyped as denoting servility, but Islamic law has made thousands of women very rich through inheritance sharing. According to Cowan (1978), "their women cover themselves with modesty, but have a powerful, seductive, and controlling role in the well-being of their society. Ours have burned their bras but have a less than powerful role in American society. Their women are adored and praised for their contributions and insights. Here, she is treated as an object and becomes the butt of dirty jokes. Professional women are beginning to be welcomed in Middle Eastern affairs as a source of talent and skill . . . [Here, they] are accepted, but reluctantly and with suspicion, often perceived in competitive terms, as a threat" (p. 9).

A Few Differences

Below is a list of some major differences between the Saudi-Arab and American cultures.

Saudi-Arab culture	American culture
Language	*Language*
• three major dialects: Hijazi (most used), Najdi, Shargi	• English
Religion	*Religion*
• church and state are one	• separation of church and state
• rules every aspect of daily life	• religion is private
• belief in set destiny and stoicism	• beliefs vary
Government	*Government*
• kingdom	• democratic republic
• strict laws and swift punishment	• moderate code with extended appeals process
• people ruled by king and his brothers	• elected president and representatives
• demands duty and obligation to the state social model: stability and long history	• freedom of individual: continuous change and short history
General	*General*
• easy pace	• fast pace and always active
• dislike of personal conflict	• more direct and abrasive
• streets are noisy and chaotic	• streets are clean and orderly
• time is indeterminate	• time is precisely measured
• economy based almost uniquely on oil and petrochemicals	• multiple and varied industries

Saudi-Arab culture	American culture
Social relations	*Social relations*
• preference for being surrounded by friends, neighbors, and family	• privacy held dear
• face and personal relations are very important	• competence and efficiency highly valued
• easily affected by public criticism	• accustomed to open and direct criticism
• courteous and polite in the house	• extends courteous manners outside the home
• normally do not respond negatively	• more direct
• a tendency for exaggeration and bragging	• preference for modesty and understatement
• women not normally included in male circle of friends	• men and women generally accepted by both
• relationships to women have to do with marriage, sex, or family	• relationships to women include as friends and coworkers, as well as relationships based on marriage, sex, or family
World of work	*World of work*
• contacts sought and used to advantage	• use of personal contacts viewed as suspect
• nepotism and loyalty to friends are characteristic	• nepotism and loyalty to friends are frowned upon
• lack of enthusiasm and initiative	• motivated by search for material well-being and being able to organize
Family	*Family*
• extended	• nuclear
• happiness and tranquility promoted	• self-reliance and competition promoted
• generations housed together	• generations reside in separate apartments or houses

Saudi-Arab culture	**American culture**
Women	*Women*
• veiled, respected, protected	• liberated, self-reliant
• talent and skill becoming recognized	• accepted reluctantly and as competition
• insightfulness and contributions lauded	• often overlooked and seen as sex objects
Education	*Education*
• separate schools for males and females	• mostly co-educational
• growth in schools for women	• number of women's schools has decreased
• growth of higher education	• higher education remains at approximately 3,000 institutions
• schooling traditional	• schooling is open to all approaches

THE NEW SOCIAL ORDER

A recent publication by Ibrahim (1982) looks at the impact of oil wealth on Arab society, which he aptly designates as the new Arab social order, a "constant internal motion" (p. 2), as "oil and movement of manpower and money across country lines is one of the Arab World's silent revolutions" (p. 3).

Here is what has been happening in this new social order. Bedouins have accepted that which is compatible with tradition. In addition, the incidence of alcoholism and divorce are definitely increasing; so is drug use among youth and some growing resistance to authority. The oil impact has produced a new type of businessman who is well educated and who knows his way around in both the oil industry and government circles; brokerage and subcontracting are his forte. It should also be mentioned that there are many others who have proved to be quite artful in taking advantage of developments in their surroundings; the word *al-kafil* is used to describe them. Finally, a new breed has been born, which Ibrahim (1982) calls "the angry Muslim militant" who is seeking more independence and social justice.

The social order is also being affected by the influx of migrants from other Arab countries who are steadily becoming more numerous than the natives, bringing in new and different ideas and subcultures, and effecting a more global outlook. This migration has given more responsibility to women at home and has brought more women from different countries into Saudi Arabia.

For the Saudi rulers, the migration of Arab minorities, Asians, and Westerners has brought about many changes, some of which are briefly mentioned here. Saudis now have new styles, social problems, changing views, altered mores, new ideas not always in consonance with those of the older generation, and greater contact with the ways and peoples of different parts of the world. Migration and change have also given rise to concerns regarding the mounting costs of growth and internal security; the steady erosion of Islamic standards, culture, and work practices; the more vocal questioning of the present socio-political system; and the dissatisfaction of purists of all ages. More changes are in the offing, as the Saudis feel the ever-mounting impact not only of the migrants but also of the world's fluctuating oil needs, the power struggle in the Middle East and foreign entanglements in trade and industry. As Ibrahim (1982) states, "the flux of such large-scale heterogeneous population into a fragile and basically conservative social structure was bound to create all types of stress and strain . . ." (p. 120).

"He who only knows his country is like a man who reads but the first chapter of a book" (St. Augustine).

REFERENCES

Alnimir, Saud Mohammad, 1981. "Present and Future Bureaucrats in Saudi Arabia: A Survey Research." Ph.D. Dissertation, Florida State University.

Althen, Gary L. (ed.), 1978. *Students from the Arab World and Iran.* Washington, D.C.: National Association for Foreign Student Affairs.

Bagnole, John W., 1976. *TEFL, Perceptions, and the Arab World.* Occasional Paper Number Three. Washington, D.C.: American Friends of the Middle East, Inc.

Brooks, Nelson, 1968. "Teaching Culture in the Foreign Language Classroom." Foreign Language Annals 1, 3. March: 204N17.

Cleveland, Alice Ann, Jean Craven, and Maryanne Danfelser, 1979. "Universals of Culture." *Intercom* (May).

Cowan, James, 1967. "Factors Influencing Arab and Iranian Students—In Country and In the United States." In *Students from the Arab World and Iran,* edited by Gary Althen. Washington, D.C.: NAFSA: 1–13.

Ibrahim, Saad Eddin, 1982. *The New Arab Social Order: A Study of the Social Impact of Oil Wealth.* Boulder, CO: Westview Press, Inc.

Lacey, Robert, 1981. *The Kingdom: Arabia and the House of Saud.* New York: Avon Books.

Lee, Eve, 1980. *The American in Saudi Arabia.* Chicago, IL: Intercultural Press, Inc.

Murdock, George P., et al., 1980. *Outline of Cultural Materials* (rev. ed.). New Haven: Human Relations Area File.

Nostrand, Howard L., 1973. *The "Emergent Model."* Seattle, WA: University of Washington.

Sefein, Naim A., 1981. "Islamic Beliefs and Practices." *The Social Studies* 72, 4 (July–August): 158–64.

Thompson, J. H., and R. D. Reischauer (eds.), 1966. *Modernization of the Arab World.* New York: D. Van Nostrand Co., Inc.

Cultural Factors Evolving from the Notional-Functional Approach

CHARLES M. BAILEY

THIS ARTICLE ADDRESSES the impact of cultural factors on the applicability of the notional-functional approach in the teaching of English as a second language to Portuguese immigrants in New Bedford, Massachusetts. We will look at the attitudes, values, and needs of the Portuguese immigrant and discuss the value of the notional-functional approach in teaching English to this group. It is the author's intent to show that the notional-functional approach is culturally appropriate for use with this group. A brief survey of the notional-functional approach will be given, followed by a discussion of this particular ethnic group and the implementation of this approach in assisting them to learn English.

The major characteristic of the notional-functional approach to language teaching is its sensitivity to individual needs. Many methodologies ignore the fact that the primary goal of second language learning is the ability to use real, appropriate language to communicate and interact with others. The organization and design of a curriculum that uses a notional-functional approach contribute to the goal of communication and interaction from the first day of study—at whatever age or learning level.

The notional-functional approach springs from an attempt to classify exactly what aspects of a language have been mastered by a particular student. The early work in this area was concerned with suitable bases for such a classification. Proponents of this method suggest that language is much more appropriately classified in terms of what people want to do with it (functions) or what meanings people want to convey (notions) than in terms of grammatical items, as in traditional language teaching models. We all understand that language is used to apologize, greet, persuade, recommend, or praise, and we all understand that language is used to express certain meanings, time, or spatial relations; but we do not all agree that we use language to exemplify grammatical categories invented by linguists. Thus, a notional-functional organization of language teaching incorporates a classification which closely matches ordinary people's perception of the purpose of language.

A notional-functional approach to language learning places major emphasis on the communicative purpose(s) of a speech act. It focuses on what people want to do or accomplish through speech. Do they want to talk about a picture, a book, a film, or something in the room they are in? Do they want to give in to their creative impulses and write a poem? These are simple examples of the functions of language which all human beings wish to express at one time or other. We try to let others know our purpose or aim in speaking in the first place.

Functional language must also incorporate specific notions; e.g., the vocabulary items in the sentence "I'd like to invite you over to my house for dinner" might answer the questions *who, when, where,* and *why.* Words following the specific functional expression would generally be considered notions. Thus, *notions* are meaning elements which may be expressed through nouns, pronouns, verbs, prepositions, conjunctions, adjectives, or adverbs.

Current proponents of the notional-functional approach (Finocchiaro and Brumfit 1983) point out the existence of a cultural component within the approach. This is extremely important, for we as language teachers know that when we are teaching language, we are teaching culture at the same time. While the learning of linguistic forms could happen over a definite period of time, far more time is necessary to acquire enough knowledge about the culture of the target community to participate fully in conversations. Parts of messages in oral or written communication are misunderstood or given false values because sociocultural experiences have not been shared by listener and speaker, or writer and reader. Gestures and facial expressions may be especially difficult for the nonnative speaker to decipher, and all language operates within a network of meanings signaled by clothes, architecture, and other cultural conventions.

Cultural immersion is simply not enough to overcome this gap, unless newcomers receive a tremendous amount of varied and natural input from near-native or native speakers of the target language and culture (Krashen 1981). Explicit information will be needed, especially if newcomers to the target country live and work in areas where they continue to hear their native language. If explicit information is not given, newcomers may spend years learning the significance of gestures, distances, or cultural allusions.

A notional-functional curriculum provides for the implicit and explicit learning of culture and language varieties through a multimedia approach, and an active methodology based on creative use of language. Where feasible, radio broadcasts, television, tapes, cassettes, documentary and recreational films, and pictures of all kinds, as well as short illustrated dialogues in a variety of everyday, real-life situations are included in the curriculum.

In the matter of cultural allusions, paralinguistic features of languages (tone of voice, groans, sighs, and other unarticulated sounds), and kinesics, the curriculum should set realistic objectives. Learners, particularly prospective U.S. immigrants, should be given basic cultural insights, facts for immediate recognition and use in their native tongue, and thus the potential for continuing their study through observation while studying, working, and living with native speakers in the new community. An excellent presentation of the cultural component of the notional-functional approach is further discussed in Finocchiaro and Brumfit (1983: 128-132).

THE SITUATION IN NEW BEDFORD

Over 35 percent of the population of men in Portugal immigrate to other areas of the world. Many of them come to the U.S., bringing with them their wives and children. Many of these families have settled in the port city of New Bedford, Massachusetts. This city has the largest cohesive Portuguese community in America; in 1965, 50 percent of the city's population was of Portuguese origin, largely first- and second-generation Americans who still had known relatives in Portugal. The enactment of the Immigration and Nationality Act of 1965 has resulted in the immigration of some 20,000 persons annually from Portugal to the U.S., 80 percent of whom settle in southeastern New England (principally in the cities of Providence, Fall River, and New Bedford). Thus, in New Bedford there is a firmly established, cohesive, ethnic subcommunity. Its continuation and replenishment since the mid-1960s, and the revisions of the immigration statutes, have necessitated a continuing programmatic effort by the schools to meet the needs of the non-English-speaking immigrant (Corasco 1972).

The aspirations of most Portuguese immigrants are to become

mainstream Americans and to be integrated into American society as quickly as possible (personal communication with Dr. Maria Brisk, 1984). To do this they must learn English. The context of learning English for Portuguese immigrants is within the American culture. As Brown (1980) states, "this clearly involves the deepest form of acculturation. The learner must survive within a strange culture as well as learn a language on which he is totally dependent for communication" (p. 130).

Practically all of the immigrants who come to the U.S. are in search of jobs, and their primary educational need is to learn job-specific English. Maria Brisk, who works with Portuguese immigrants, says that "the best result so far with teaching English to the Portuguese immigrants has been to implement a vocationally oriented track (VESL) dealing with such things as the restaurant world, food, tourists, etc., in the language learning curriculum." She also says, "these people have very little time in which to learn English. Most of them work all day and go to school at night" (personal communication, 1984). What method, then, would be the most appropriate in meeting the educational needs of the immigrant and at the same time facilitating the acculturation process?

With no specific modifications for the teaching of English and North American culture to the Portuguese, the notional-functional approach is very suitable in meeting the needs of this particular group here in the U.S. Portuguese who have had some education are used to a regimented and disciplined school setup. Unless things are presented to them in a very clear, dogmatic fashion, there won't be much learning (Macedo, personal communication, 1984). This seems to rule out the use of innovative techniques for language learning (Suggestopedia, The Silent Way, etc.). Macedo (1984) has serious doubts about how much Portuguese immigrants would benefit from these methods. He states that "they [the immigrants] have to have a well-structured kind of language learning situation." Macedo's experience using the notional-functional approach to teach English to these immigrants has been very positive. He says, "it works in any situation, whether the immigrant is educated or not. It especially works for people who have to work for a living and don't have much time to fool around" (personal communication, 1984).

In addition to teaching English through the notional-functional approach, it is also possible to teach the culture of North America through the use of this method. The notional-functional approach gives more elasticity to the acculturation process and can even reduce the experience of culture shock.

Throughout the centuries, the Portuguese in foreign situations have shown extreme adaptability and flexibility, to the extent that they often give up their own culture. Brisk (personal communication, 1984) says that one important prerequisite for social and economic success for the Portuguese-American is better integration into the value system of the larger Anglo society. If necessary, this integration should come about with loss of loyalty to the old Portuguese culture. Brisk was surprised when she saw how quickly the immigrants change their values and attitudes, rapidly assimilating or melting into American society. She says, "they love the idea of becoming natives; there is no resistance on their part to do so" (personal communication, 1984). This feeling is prevalent among old and young alike—the younger generation being the carrier of the future of the ethnic group and the conveyer of values to their offspring.

The author asked Dr. Richard Preto-Rodas, who has had vast experience with Portuguese immigrants, to compare them to Puerto Rican immigrants, hoping to find some similarities in the group experience. He stated that, "unlike the Puerto Rican situation, the Portuguese situation is new for this hemisphere. One is dealing with a totally different mentality. The Portuguese situation is closely related to that of the Vietnamese situation. Both of these groups have a much more ingrained reverence and respect for the teacher who is the authority figure. In other words, they have much more shared values with respect to concepts of teacher and classroom than do similar versus with the Puerto Ricans," (Richard Preto-Rodas, personal communication, 1984).

Most immigrants who come to the United States looking for jobs need to be taught immediate linguistic and cultural skills so that they may function within a society which is predominantly English-speaking. The notional-functional approach is an excellent one for acquiring basic functional and survival skills in the new culture. The Portuguese are good students in traditional classroom situations, but in most innovative situations they would do very poorly. The notional-functional approach is not experimental; it is a cut-and-dried approach which may fulfill the needs of most immigrants. The teacher should find very little resistance on the part of the Portuguese to learning English and the American way of life.

REFERENCES

Brown, H. Douglas, 1980. *Principles of Language Learning and Teaching*. Englewood Cliffs, N.J.: Prentice-Hall.

Brumfit, Christopher, and Mary Finocchiaro, 1983. *The Notional-Functional Approach.* New York: Oxford University Press.

DeSilva, Joao Fernandes, 1980. "Aspects of Education in Portugal." *Western European Education* 12, 4 (Winter): 88–95.

Krashen, Stephen D., 1981. *Second Language Acquisition and Second Language Learning.* New York: Oxford University Press.

Cultural Aspects in the Development of Reading Comprehension Skills

Luz Paredes Lono

THE TEACHING OF READING is of utmost importance in ESL academically oriented programs. Foreign students who want to study in American universities need to read fairly fast and achieve a high degree of comprehension to keep up with reading assignments and succeed in school.

Reading comprehension is difficult to attain because the reading activity in itself is complex. It is possible to identify the numerous aspects involved in obtaining information from the printed page, but it is more difficult to determine precisely what strategies good readers use or how they select them. The complexity of achieving full comprehension lies in the fact that reading involves not just linguistic but also cultural aspects. Both must be addressed in the reading class.

Cultural elements, implicitly or explicitly stated in reading selections, can pose serious problems to foreign students who attempt to decode the language and understand every word they read. Teachers cannot assume that their students will be able to understand reading material on their own, in spite of the cultural elements.

The need to deal with cultural information in the reading class has been pointed out by several researchers. Carolyn Ebel (1978) conducted a study on reading practices in elementary bilingual schools throughout the United States. She discovered that although teachers were aware of the existence of cultural differences among students and of the need to understand these better, they did not realize how much students' cultural backgrounds affect their comprehension. She also discovered that teachers make sparse use of materials containing culturally relevant information. According to Ebel, students with limited relevant information can't predict or understand what they read. Furthermore, she points out that retention of words is greatly influenced by the reader's experience with them.

Ronald Wardaugh (1969) has identified "contextual-pragmatic knowledge" as one of the essential components of the reading activity. According to him, in order to interpret a passage, readers have to have knowledge and understanding of the world around them. Personal experience in that world, of course, is essential. Students who lack the cultural experience discussed or presented in the reading will fail to understand and react to it appropriately.

A psycholinguistic model for reading comprehension has been presented by James Coady (1979), who views reading as the result of interaction among conceptual abilities, background knowledge, and process strategies. The background knowledge component, he states, becomes an important element affecting the speed with which students learn English: "Students with a Western background of some kind learn English faster, on the average, than those without such a background." He also indicates that one pedagogical implication from his reading model is that "the ESL student should take advantage of his strengths in order to overcome his weaknesses. For example, greater background knowledge of a particular subject matter could compensate somewhat for a lack of syntactic control over the language."

The importance of culture in the reading comprehension process has also been pointed out by David E. Eskey (1979). His reading model includes both a cultural and a language component. According to him, problems in reading comprehension are caused by the difficulty of the language in terms of its syntax and vocabulary, and by the cultural concepts and rhetorical organization embedded in every reading passage. Other studies conducted by Patricia Carrell (1984), Carrell and Wallace (1982), and Carrell and Eisterhold (1983) have focused on the importance of background knowledge in the reading comprehension process of ESL students within the framework of schema theory.

The models for reading comprehension mentioned above direct ESL teachers to deal with cultural aspects in a direct and systematic way in the reading class. They also emphasize that reading comprehension requires active participation by the reader.

Three main aspects will be addressed here. The first one will deal with schema theory and how the reading process is viewed within that framework. The second will deal with different levels of reading comprehension ESL students should attain. The third will deal with a few strategies that ESL teachers should use to help students improve their reading skills.

SCHEMA THEORY

Being able to identify and interpret the graphic symbols used in English (the linguistic code) and understand word meanings used in various syntactic structures is an essential part of the reading process. However, that is not all reading comprehension is about. Comprehension implies understanding the overall message, above and beyond the literal meaning of the words used in a reading passage. It also includes understanding of concepts such as family, education, and religion, which may involve dimensions that are difficult for foreign students to understand because they are different from those in their own cultures.

The study of how reading comprehension takes place leads us to the study of schema theory. In this theoretical model of reading, the reader is as important as the text; reading is viewed as an interactive process between the text and the reader's background knowledge (Carrell and Eisterhold 1983). Comprehension takes place when the information provided in the text triggers a response from the reader whose background knowledge has been activated. Carrell and Eisterhold (1983) indicate that "according to schema theory the process of interpretation is guided by the principle that every input is mapped against some existing schema and that all aspects of that schema must be compatible with the input information."

David E. Rumelhart (1984) defines schema theory as "a theory about how knowledge is represented and about how that representation facilitates the use of the knowledge in particular ways." Within the framework of this theory, he states, all knowledge is packaged into units which are called schemata. Rumelhart points out that a schema constitutes a data structure which represents the generic concepts that we store in memory. "There are schemata representing our knowledge about all concepts: underlying objects, situations, events, sequences of events, actions, and sequences of actions. As part of its specification, schema contains the network of interrelations believed to normally hold among the constituents of the concept of question. A schema theory embodies a *prototype* theory of meaning."

According to Rumelhart (1984), schemata have two functions, the most important being the construction of an interpretation of an event, object, or situation. Thus, a reader has comprehended the text when his or her schema helps interpret it appropriately. If this schema is different or if aspects of it cannot account for events described in the text, the reader may have to look for other ways of interpreting the information. A second function of schemata is that of predicting events that have not been observed. "We use our theories to make inferences with some confidence about these unobserved events" (Rumelhart 1984). Rumelhart provides the example of the automobile. Once we see one, we automatically assume that it has all the components an automobile usually has, even though we have not seen them or checked them ourselves.

According to schema theory, information is processed in two ways which have to occur simultaneously for comprehension of a text to take place. These are identified as bottom-up and top-down. Carrell and Eisterhold (1983) discuss these two modes in detail. They specify that schemata are organized hierarchically, with specific information at the bottom and more general information at the top. When information is received, it activates schemata at the bottom of that hierarchy and subsequently others at higher levels. This is identified as a data-driven process. On the other hand, top-down processing takes place when the reader makes general predictions about the text being read. This is identified as a conceptually driven process. "Bottom-up processing ensures that the listeners/readers will be sensitive to information that is novel or that does not fit their ongoing hypotheses about the content or structure of the text; top-down processing helps the listeners/readers to resolve ambiguities or to select between alternative possible interpretations of the incoming data" (Carrell and Eisterhold 1983).

There are two types of schemata: formal and content. Formal schemata refer to the different ways in which information is organized in different texts, the knowledge of the rhetorical patterns of organization used in presenting information. Content schemata refer to the knowledge the reader has about a specific topic. The topic may include references to holiday, tradition, etc. (Carrell and Eisterhold 1983). Thus, students may fail to understand a text because their content or formal schemata were not activated, or because they did not exist.

Students may have difficulty understanding a reading passage because it contains concepts and cultural aspects that are nonexistent in their language and culture. Equally troubling can be the fact that students may understand only some of the dimensions of the concept but not all of them. For example, when dealing with the concept of justice, students may say that they understand it because there is an equivalent word in their language. However, what justice entails in two different cultures may be miles apart. How is justice enforced, and by whom? What penalties are applied for what types of crimes? Who participates in sentencing law offenders? Is a person innocent until proven guilty, or is the opposite the case? This example provides a glimpse at the problems involved. When foreign students are asked comprehension questions in which they have to express an opinion or evaluate a situation described in a passage, they tend to answer from the point of view of their own culture. Thus, they may misunderstand the point in English.

In her study of the Chinese ESL reader, Mary Lee Field (1985) reports that "Chinese schools emphasize reading of literature as a way of learning a language, and Chinese students are eager to read and understand all of American culture." According to her, difficulties arise out of the cultural assumptions and expectations that the readers bring to the literature. She points out that "Chinese novels and stories have a markedly different literary tradition of rhetorical and narrative conventions that shape Chinese readers' expectations" (1985). A crucial point for Chinese readers is that they bring very little background knowledge to the reading task since they have very limited access to Western culture. Often, this leads them to make wrong assumptions about American life.

Part of the problem in terms of reading comprehension is that writers make assumptions about the cultural background of their readers; they assume a common cultural background that will allow readers to understand information and interpret it correctly. Tucker and Gatbonton (1971) point out that since not everything is specifically stated in a passage, students of literature many times fail to understand American values, or interpret them according to their own culture. A reader needs to capture the author's world in order to interpret it correctly. Eskey (1979) points out that for readers to understand what they read, they must have access to the writer's underlying assumptions about the subject and the world. Everything a person questions, values, and takes for granted varies from culture to culture. Foreign students, therefore, cannot be expected to predict or infer from reading material when their content schemata are not properly activated or are nonexistent.

Formal schemata refer to the rhetorical patterns of organization. Carrell (1984) has done research on the effects that different types of organization have on ESL readers. She used Meyer's five basic types of expository organization: collection, description, causation, problem/solution, and comparison, noting that

> These five basic expository types are common in various contexts. Political essays are often of the comparison type—in particular, the adversative sub-type. News articles are typically of

the description type—telling us who, what, where, when, and how. Scientific texts are often of the problem/solution type—first raising a problem and then presenting the solution. Experimental psychological research reports, such as this one, follow a specific version of the problem/solution plan—having well marked sections for the problem, method, results, and discussion. History texts often follow the time sequence type of collection.

In her 1984 study, Carrell points out that the formal schemata that correspond to the "more highly structured types of discourse (comparison, problem/solution, and causation)" will facilitate a reader's encoding, retention, and retrieval of information. Thus, identifying the rhetorical organization of a text seems to be of extreme importance in the reading comprehension process.

Language and culture are so closely intertwined that it is impossible to separate one from the other. Alexander (1969) affirms that our thoughts are oriented toward certain distinctions which are forced upon us by language and that these orientations are often below the level of awareness. Saville-Troike (1976) says that language is the expressive dimension of culture and the primary medium for its transmission. According to her, when we teach ESL, we do not teach "an alternative set of labels for the same reality, but culturally different patterns of perception, of communication and of affect." This has also been emphasized by Harris and Moran (1979), who point out that "an individual's self image, needs, values, expectations, goals, standards, cultural norms and perception have an effect on the way input is received and interpreted."

Since understanding a reading passage means understanding both the linguistic code and the culture of English speaking people, ESL teachers have to work at enhancing their students' knowledge of those areas. There is a definite need for students to develop appropriate schemata for dealing with a new language and culture.

LEVELS OF READING COMPREHENSION

Foreign students need to acquire different levels of comprehension in reading, depending not only on the difficulty of the material they are to read but also on the amount of culturally loaded information in it for which they have no point of reference. The levels of comprehension identified in the literature are factual, inference, evaluation, and application.

Students are usually able to understand passages that contain a lot of factual information: dates, names of cities, countries, people, or events. When students are asked questions about the reading, they go back over the material and recognize the information needed. Retrieval of information specifically stated, recalling events in a specific sequence, and following basic instructions are characteristic of the basic level of comprehension. Factual or literal comprehension, therefore, is perhaps the most frequent level at which instructors ask questions, despite the fact that their students may be able to handle more difficult tasks. Providing correct answers to questions eliciting literal information is no guarantee of full comprehension of the reading passage, however. Teachers need to challenge their students into using higher cognitive abilities or more difficult thinking procedures.

Questions that elicit factual information are WH-questions: *who?*, *what?*, *when?*, *where?* A good discussion of this type of question used in reading can be found in Norris (1972). According to Norris, the ESL teacher should use more questions with *how?* and *why?*, in which students are forced to go beyond the text to provide an answer. Comprehension questions, therefore, should have a natural progression from understanding facts to reaching conclusions and forming opinions. This way, students will demonstrate whether they have developed their skills.

A second level of comprehension is that of inferring information which is not specifically stated. In such a task, teachers ask students to establish relationships among different pieces of information included in the reading selection. To do this, foreign students have to realize that there are hidden messages in what the author has written. Writers do not necessarily say openly what they mean. Sometimes, by avoiding taking a position, they may let the reader know what their position is on a particular issue. Many ESL students may have trouble understanding what it is that they are supposed to relate. Arabic-speaking students, for example, have great difficulty in perceiving cause and effect relationships. Yorkey (1977) discusses the subject when he analyzes these students' difficulties in writing. This source of difficulty can also occur in reading. According to Yorkey (1977), "The unusual emphasis in Arabic on coordination rather than on subordination causes students to underestimate the importance in English of the distinction between cause and effect, real and unreal conditions, and main ideas and supporting ideas." It is not difficult to conclude from this that if students cannot see these relationships or understand them, it will be impossible for them to infer correctly, especially when this information is implicit in a passage.

It is even more difficult for ESL students to make cultural inferences when a reading passage includes descriptions of body language, proxemics, etc. Unless students are alerted to what those gestures mean, they will not be able to interpret correctly what the characters' reactions in the reading mean. Questions like "What caused Ms. X to react the way she did?" "Why was Ms. X annoyed?" "Was Ms. X impatient during the meeting? Why?" will force the student to look at behavior being described in the reading.

In her study of the effects of building background knowledge on reading comprehension, Johnson (1982) analyzed the kinds of inferences made by Iranian students. She classified the answers into two groups: compatible and incompatible. In the first group, she included summary statements, textual implications, and elaborations of information. In the second group, she included distortions of the reading due to misunderstanding of textual implications, lack of background cultural knowledge, or a culturally based misinterpretation of the passage.

The passage Johnson (1982) used dealt with Halloween. It consisted of five paragraphs, of which paragraphs one, two, and five included familiar information about description of costumes, masks, and the trick-or-treat tradition; description of the witch; and comparison of Halloween today with the past. Paragraphs three and four included unfamiliar information: celebration of Halloween in the past; and different degrees of witchcraft at that time. Johnson found out that students made correct cultural inferences when they referred to the familiar section or to their personal experience about this holiday. However, when they referred to the unfamiliar section, they made wrong inferences. This led her to conclude that "familiarity with a foreign culturally related topic, knowledge obtained from real experiences in the foreign culture is effective for reading comprehension of a passage on that topic." In a previous article, Johnson (1981) had arrived at the same conclusion. When talking about cultural inferences, she said that "the subject might elaborate on the story of the same cultural background from the perspective of the native culture." On the other hand, "the subject might distort the story of foreign cultural background because of lack of knowledge of the foreign culture" (Johnson 1981).

For a foreign student, everything in a selection might be new: the situation described, the language in which it is done, and the organization of the information. The simplest passage can be misinterpreted. For example, in reading about an American family, foreign students may infer that parents do not care about their children because they pressure them into going away to college, getting a job in a different place, or moving to their own living quarters. Some foreign students do not have a clear concept of the values and expectations of American parents. Acquiring such knowledge will prevent them from making wrong inferences. If we were to ask students to predict the outcome of a story including these cultural elements, they would probably predict it based on what would be logical in terms of their own expectations, values, and interests.

The third level of comprehension is called evaluation. It presupposes the existence of rules or characteristics against which students' ideas, actions, or thoughts are measured. Familiarity with this procedure cannot be taken for granted, especially if students come from a culture where little evaluation, but a lot of memorization, is done. Evaluation requires that the student pay attention both to the form and to the content. Of course, if the content is unfamiliar, it would be very difficult for students to evaluate the passage. They might take for granted that the concepts presented are clear and correct, and they might not question the rhetorical organization of the information.

Putting into practice what has been learned or understood through reading is difficult for foreign students. This level is called application. Students are expected to recognize valid applications of a person's ideas. They have to realize that what is concluded about one group is not necessarily applicable to other groups. For example, conclusions made about children do not apply to adolescents or adults, and conclusions about the rural population do not apply to the urban population. In reference to specific cultural aspects, students should be able to learn certain behavior through reading to facilitate their social adjustment in this country.

The comprehension levels mentioned above are closely related to specific thinking processes: concrete thinking, categorizing, deduction, induction, and prediction (Friedman and Rowls 1980). In dealing with *concrete thinking*, students need practice in recalling specific information, following directions, paraphrasing, and recalling a sequence of events. *Categorizing* implies classification of ideas and differentiation between fact and opinion, real and unreal, relevant and irrelevant, evaluating reading, and integrating old and new information. *Deductive reasoning* requires practice in identifying supportive information and details, inferring details, analyzing conclusions, providing examples and illustrations, and application of information. *Inductive reasoning* is acquired through practice in summarizing stories, getting the main idea, generalizing and interpreting the author's style, mood, and purpose. Finally, *prediction* requires that students make hypotheses that they will have to prove or reject as they continue reading, that they forecast and predict story outcomes and anticipate what will happen next. This corresponds to what Goodman (1967) identified as "a psycholinguistic guessing game."

It is important to be aware that foreign students may not be familiar with the way information is organized in English. If both the content of the story (content schemata) and the type of rhetorical organization (formal schemata) are new to them, students will have trouble achieving full comprehension of a reading passage.

Techniques to Help Students Improve their Reading Skills

Once teachers realize that students lack the cultural experience to understand many reading passages, they should take the responsibility of helping students acquire that background knowledge through personal experience. They may offer actual exposure to that which is presented in the reading, through presentation, explanation, or role-playing. Role-playing allows students to pretend they are different people in a different setting. In this way, they can experience new cultural aspects before reading about them.

Selekman and Kleinman (1978) developed a special technique called "communicative interaction," in which socio-cultural aspects of a reading passage were actually experienced by the readers. The reading passage Selekman and Kleinman selected dealt with astronauts on the moon and their sense of loneliness and alienation. In the passage, references were made to the things the astronauts missed most from the Earth. The interaction Selekman and Kleinman described involved separate but specific steps. First of all, in order to understand how the astronauts felt, students had to find out what things the astronauts missed and for what reasons. Thus, students were asked to tell of things they missed about their own country while they were in the United States. Then they were asked to pretend they were Americans studying in a foreign country and figure out what they would miss. After the role-playing, a brief discussion took place, dealing with the emotional involvement and recognition of underlying sociological information. The key to the experience was for students to explore their own feelings and thus be better equipped to understand the reading passage.

In their discussion of role-playing and its advantages, Donahue and Parsons (1982) mention that it "provides a sensitizing situation in which the students work as a group to develop awareness and understanding of other cultures. Students have an opportunity to view the comments of others in a situation objectively. They learn to listen and watch another person before responding."

Teachers need to concentrate on both the content of a reading and its organization. Recognition of the rhetorical patterns of organization will help students acquire formal schemata. In her discussion of the effects of rhetorical organization on ESL readers, Carrell (1984) says that "devoting reading instruction to the identification of different discourse structures may be effective in facilitating reading comprehension, retention and recall." Studies in contrastive rhetoric also seem to point out that foreign students need to familiarize themselves with the way information is conveyed in English. Kaplan (1980) has pointed out that logic is not universal; it "varies from culture to culture and even from time to time within a given culture." Kaplan also points out that the thought patterns readers of English expect are "linear in their development." Paragraphs usually start with a topic sentence followed by several subdivisions which are supported by examples and illustrations. This is how the central idea is developed and related to the rest of the essay.

However, information may be conveyed differently in other languages. Kaplan (1980) suggests that "In the teaching of paragraph structure to foreign students, whether in terms of reading or in terms of composition, the teacher must be himself aware of these differences, and he must make these differences overtly apparent to his students." Furthermore, Kaplan (1980) says that foreign students need to understand the cultural aspects of logic on which rhetorical structures are based to "bring the student not only to an understanding of contrastive grammar and a new vocabulary, which are parts of any reading task, but also to a grasp of idea and structure in units larger than a sentence."

Teachers need to help students read critically. They should teach students to evaluate the merits of statements made in newspaper and magazine articles. For this purpose, teachers can use editorials from two newspapers which present different points of view on the same issue. Students should be taught how to evaluate the arguments presented and how to locate key information in the text that will help them decide for or against one of the positions. Basically, students should be taught not to take for granted that all information in print is good, accurate, or unbiased.

Newspapers also offer a good opportunity for foreign students to learn about American culture, not only in terms of the information available in them, but also in terms of what they reflect about Americans' interests. Blatchford (1973) states that "In terms of language skills, there is plenty to talk about or recognize in the different registers of English and the appropriate use of each. Activities which emanate from a newspaper class can center around a cultural theme, but give practice in the language. The discussion of cultural differences practices speaking; the discussion itself involves comprehension; understanding the topic under discussion involves reading." Teachers can also use advertisements to teach their students to distinguish between fact and opinion, to identify the people advertisements appeal to, and to draw conclusions about the claims ads make.

Teachers need to concentrate their efforts on asking questions that make use of progressively more difficult thinking processes. Inference and evaluation should be emphasized over retrieval of facts and dates. Open-ended questions are excellent means of accomplishing this.

Teachers also need to discuss, explain, and introduce new concepts and culturally loaded information before the reading takes place. This will help students to achieve a higher degree of comprehension. ESL students should be encouraged to predict outcomes in the stories they read. This forces them to process both linguistic and cultural information to predict accurately.

Since reading skills improve with practice, teachers need to encourage students to read outside of class as much as they can. Topics that are related to ones read in class will offer students the opportunity to expand their knowledge about a particular subject and avoid some cultural comprehension problems that have already been dealt with. This will also give readers a sense of accomplishment because they will be able to relate the material to their new schemata.

At the advanced level, teachers may use literature effectively to help their students understand American culture. Sandra McKay (1982) discusses the pros and cons of using literature in the ESL classroom and concludes that "It can be useful in developing linguistic knowledge both on a usage and use level. Secondly, to the extent that students enjoy reading literature, it may increase their motivation to interact with a text and, thus, ultimately increase their reading proficiency. Finally, an examination of a foreign culture through literature may increase their understanding of that culture and perhaps spur their own creation of imaginative works." This, she points out, will depend on the effective selection of textbooks which should be adequate both on the linguistic and conceptual level.

In conclusion, ESL teachers need to introduce cultural aspects regularly. Pre-reading and post-reading activities will help foreign students clarify concepts and acquire new insights into the American culture. In a multicultural, multilingual class, we cannot expect ESL teachers to know all their students' cultures thoroughly, but there is no excuse for not being aware of their own. Teachers should also make sure that their students understand the skills they are learning and the problems they must overcome in order to achieve full comprehension in reading.

References

Alexander, Hubert G., 1969. *Meaning in Language*. Glenview, IL: Scott, Foresman and Company.
Blatchford, Charles H., 1973. "Newspapers: Vehicles for Teaching ESOL with a Cultural Focus." *TESOL Quarterly* 7:2 (June).

Carrell, Patricia L., 1984. "The Effects of Rhetorical Organization on ESL Reader Readers." *TESOL Quarterly* 18:3 (Sept.).

Carrell, Patricia L., and Joan C. Eisterhold, 1983. "Schema Theory and ESL Reading Pedagogy." *TESOL Quarterly* 17:4 (Dec.).

Carrell, Patricia L., and Bill Wallace, 1983. "Background Knowledge: Context and Familiarity in Reading Comprehension." In *ON TESOL '82: Pacific Perspectives on Language Learning and Teaching,* edited by Mark A. Clarke and Jean Handscombe. Washington, D.C.: Teachers of English to Speakers of Other Languages.

Clarke, Mark A., and Sandra Silberstein, 1979. "Toward a Realization of Psycholinguistic Principles in the ESL Reading Class." In *Reading in a Second Language,* edited by Ronald Mackay, Bruce Barkman and R. R. Jordan. Rowley, MA: Newbury House.

Coady, James, 1979. "A Psycholinguistic Model of the ESL Reader." In *Reading in a Second Language.* Rowley, MA: Newbury House.

Donahue, Meghan, and Adelaide Heyde Parsons, 1982. "The Use of Role Play to Overcome Cultural Fatigue." *TESOL Quarterly* 16:3 (Sept.).

Ebel, Carolyn, 1978. "A study of English as a Second Language Reading Instruction in Bilingual Programs." *Nabe Journal* III: 1.

Eskey, David E., 1979. "A Model Program for Teaching Advanced Reading to Students of English as a Foreign Language." In *Reading in a Second Language.* Rowley, MA: Newbury House.

Field, Mary Lee, 1985. "A Psycholinguistic Model for the Chinese ESL Reader." In *On TESOL '84: A Brave New World for TESOL,* edited by Penny Larson, Elliot L. Judd, and Dorothy S. Messerschmitt. Washington, D.C.: Teachers of English to Speakers of Other Languages.

Friedman, Myles I., and Michael D. Rowls, 1980. *Teaching Reading and Thinking Skills.* New York: Longman, Inc.

Goodman, Kenneth S., 1967. "Reading: A Psycholinguistic Guessing Game." *Journal of the Reading Specialist,* vol. 6.

Harris, Philip R., and Robert T. Moran, 1979. *Managing Cultural Differences.* Houston: Gulf Publishing Company.

Johnson, Patricia, 1981. "Effects on Reading Comprehension of Language Complexity and Cultural Background of a Text." *TESOL Quarterly* 15:2 (June).

_____, 1982. "Effects on Reading Comprehension of Building Background Knowledge." *TESOL Quarterly* 16:4 (December).

Kaplan, Robert B., 1980. "Cultural Thought Patterns in Intercultural Education." In *Readings on English as a Second Language,* edited by Kenneth Croft. Cambridge, MA: Winthrop Publishers, Inc.

McKay, Sandra, 1982. "Literature in the ESL Classroom." *TESOL Quarterly* 16:4 (Dec.).

Norris, William E., 1972. "Advanced Reading: Goals, Techniques, Procedures." In *Readings on English as a Second Language,* edited by Kenneth Croft. Cambridge, MA: Winthrop Publishers, Inc.

Perkins, Kyle, and Barbara Jones, 1985. "Measuring Passage Contribution in ESL Reading Comprehension." *TESOL Quarterly* 19:1 (March).

Rumelhart, David E., 1977. "Understanding and Summarizing Brief Stories." In *Basic Processes in Reading: Perception and Comprehension,* edited by David La Berge and S. Jay Samuels. Hillsdale, NJ: Lawrence Erlbaum Associates.

_____, 1984. "Understanding Understanding." In *Understanding Reading Comprehension: Cognition, Language, and the Structure of Prose,* edited by James Flooded. Newark, DE: International Reading Association.

_____, 1980. "Schemata: The Building Blocks of Cognition." In *Theoretical Issues in Reading Comprehension,* edited by Rand J. Spiro, Bertram C. Bruce, and William E. Brewer. Hillsdale, NJ: Lawrence Erlbaum Associates.

Saville-Troike, Muriel, 1976. *Foundations for Teaching English as a Second Language.* Englewood Cliffs, NJ: Prentice-Hall.

Selekman, Howard R., and Howard H. Kleinman, 1978. "A Technique for Aiding Second Language Reading Comprehension." In *On TESOL '78: ESL Policies, Pro-*

grams, Practices. Washington, D.C.: Teachers of English to Speakers of Other Languages.

Tucker, R., and E. Gatbonton, 1971. "Cultural Orientation and the Study of Foreign Literature." *TESOL Quarterly* 5:2 (June).

Wardaugh, Ronald, 1969. *Reading: A Linguistic Perspective.* New York: Harcourt Brace & World.

Yorkey, Richard, 1977. "Practical EFL Techniques for Teaching Arabic-Speaking Students." In *The Human Factors in ESL,* edited by James E. Alatis and Ruth Crymes. Washington, D.C.: Teachers of English to Speakers of Other Languages.

The Need for a Cross-Cultural Component in the Education of Students in Engineering and Business

PAULA W. SUNDERMAN

ENGINEERING AND BUSINESS are popular fields of study in the United States for both American and international students. The growing number of high-tech companies in this country and the proliferation of technological advances in areas such as space exploration have led to a demand for graduates in a number of specialized fields in engineering and management. In addition, an ever-increasing need for Western technology in many Third World countries since the 1960s has resulted in a surge of international students studying engineering and other applied scientific fields in American colleges and universities. As Western technology is brought to Third World countries, there is a concomitant need for skilled managers to introduce the new technology in these countries and to ensure its successful reception among the indigenous population.

While the curricula that these students are enrolled in, whether they are American or international, stress mastery of subject matter and technical expertise, too often an important component of their education is neglected. This is the cross-cultural component, which is vital not only to their studies in the United States but also to their careers either in their home countries or in other countries. Many of these students will work abroad for multinational companies at some time in their careers. In addition to their need for technical and managerial skills, their professional success will also depend upon many factors related to culture. They will need to learn intercultural communication skills, avoidance of ethnocentrism and stereotyping, adaptability to a new culture, skill in another language, and a willingness to interact with host country nationals. Even those who remain in their own countries will not be unaffected, for they may still work for a multinational company or interact with subcultures within their own society which have different values and needs.

As Josef A. Mestenhauser (1981) points out in his article "Selected Learning Concepts and Theories" (in *Learning Across Cultures,* edited by Gary Althen), "Differentiation about American culture and society is very important to foreign students' understanding of the elements which make their academic fields uniquely 'American' or 'culture-bound,' even in the so-called hard sciences, which are not supposed to have national or cultural boundaries" (p. 120). He cogently argues that foreign students should understand the part of U.S. culture which relates to their disciplines. The reverse is true, as well. American students need to understand the cultures of other countries, for powerful cultural pressures tend to "mitigate against breaking up of accepted world views for the purpose of analysis and synthesis" (Mestenhauser, p. 120). In addition, people tend "to differentiate more in their own culture than in the second culture" and "since culture-learning is comparative, differentiation across cultures may lead to misperceptions, distortions and inaccuracies" (p. 120).

If education in the United States is to be truly international, it must provide an intercultural focus in all disciplines, from the humanities to the sciences. The increasing pressure to re-examine our international educational efforts in relation to their relevance for Third World development requires that the education and training all students receive take into account cross-cultural differences and intercultural communication.

The old adage that science and technology are culture-free may be accurate, but the engineers and managers who make decisions about the allocation of their research and its products are very much culture-bound. Working within the parameters of their own cultures, they may fail to recognize that persons of other cultures have different goals, customs, thought patterns, and values. To make decisions that do not take cultural differences into account may cause strife or the abandonment of a particular enterprise. As a result, a portion of the population may be alienated, and the company can lose not only its investment but also the good will of the local populace. Therefore, it is vital that engineers and managers be educated in intercultural relations and cross-cultural differences so that they can adapt technological advancements to a variety of cultures and circumstances.

Why the Cross-Cultural Component is Often Omitted

In many cases, colleges of engineering and business rely upon the students' employers to train them in understanding and coping with cross-cultural differences. The problem with this approach is that employees of multinational corporations seldom receive adequate instruction in intercultural relations before they are transferred overseas. While training in technological and managerial problems is commonplace, the cross-cultural component is often neglected because it is perceived as being less important than the technical skills. This is unfortunate, because instruction and training in intercultural relations can help multinational managers to meet world competition, foster cooperativeness in the workplace, and cut costs in foreign deployment. "Managers" here include engineers who hold managerial positions in multinational companies which require them to interchange on a daily basis with host internationals.

As Philip Harris and Robert Moran (1979:10) report, intercultural studies benefit employees in the following ways. They

1. Facilitate adjustment and productivity in a foreign country or at home with minority cultures.

2. Foster international goodwill and customer relations, as well as business and profits.

3. Increase human relations skills with foreigners, minorities, or ethnic group representatives.

4. Offer better understanding of both domestic and international markets and reports related thereto.

5. Provide insight relative to organizational culture and personnel behavior.

6. Sensitize management to the needs of foreign nationals on assignment to corporate home culture.

7. Assist in reentry to one's native culture and organization upon return from abroad.

8. Help one to gain a better sense of self and cultural heritage for more effective intercultural interactions.

MANAGERS AS AGENTS OF CHANGE

Managers are, by definition, agents of change. Managers (including engineers in management positions) who operate in another culture are usually introducers of a new product, service, method, or technology. Proposed changes do not take place within a vacuum; they involve human factors. How well changes can be integrated within a society or culture depends upon a variety of factors: speed of change, preparation for change, acceptance of change, and, if necessary, adaptation of the proposed change to fit the mores of that society or culture. To cite only one example, a number of developing countries desire Western technology but not Western culture. Saudi Arabia, for instance, has spent large sums of petrodollars to import Western technology. Since there was very little native infrastructure in the country to support the new technology, Western technicians had to be brought in; they, in turn, brought their own culture with them. Until enough Saudi engineers and technicians can be trained, it seems likely that Western culture will continue to enter the country with the purveyors of Western technology.

Change is often perceived as a threat by the indigenous population, particularly in the case of Western technology imposed upon a society by its managers. Those in charge of importing the technology have a number of factors to consider before implementing their projects. One of these is that Western technology in its existing form may not be appropriate to the needs of the people or the environment. For example, technology that will put people out of work as the result of its efficiency may not be desired in labor-intensive countries. Robots, popular in developed countries, would not be wanted by a local population that relies upon cheap domestic labor. Yet, too often, developing countries import Western technology without considering the cost-benefit ratio or the human factors. For instance, international students who are educated in the United States in technical and scientific fields are used to working with very sophisticated technology. However, when they return to their countries to implement the new technology, they often discover that it must first be adapted to meet local needs and circumstances.

Even the transfer of appropriate technology is not without its problems. While appropriate technology may, in the short term, benefit one group of people, it may in the long term cause social and economic problems to another group. For example, the displacement of women in some Southeast Asian countries from their traditional agricultural work by the introduction of new technology has had serious economic repercussions. Another possibility is that one socioeconomic group may benefit at the expense of another, thus widening the gap between the rich and the poor.

Among the variety of issues involved in cross-cultural relations, the following topics have particular relevance for students in engineering and business.

Intercultural communication skills

Harris and Moran (1979:19-20) mention five guidelines for helping managers develop intercultural communication skills:

1. No one can avoid communicating. That is, even when they are silent, people still communicate by means of body language, the color of their skin, the color of their clothes, or even the gifts they give. All behavior is communication, then, because all behavior contains a message, whether it is intended or not.

2. Communication does not necessarily mean understanding. Each individual brings to the communication process his or her own background, including interpretation of symbols according to a particular culture. For example, the American manager who gives a gift of white flowers in Japan has communicated, but not in the way he or she thinks; in Japan, white flowers are reserved for funerals to indicate sympathy.

3. Communication is irreversible and cannot be taken back. Trying to explain, clarify, or restate a message cannot change its effect. For example, the American manager who sharply disagrees with a Saudi Arabian employee in the presence of others has committed an "impoliteness" that will be difficult to remedy.

4. Communication occurs within a context. The context of communication which takes place at a certain time, in some place, using certain mediums, cannot be ignored. The context determines the appropriateness of the communication situation. For example, a business conversation with a French manager in France during an evening meal may be inappropriate. To immediately conduct business without first getting to know the individual with whom you are dealing is also inappropriate in Latin American and Arab countries.

5. Communication is a dynamic process. It is not static or passive, but a continuous and active process. Thus, a communicator is not simply a sender or a receiver of messages, but can be both at the same time. For instance, the way in which a receiver receives a message may send a message to the sender. What is considered a polite way of listening may vary from culture to culture, with behavior that is appropriate in one culture being deemed inappropriate in another.

The problem of effective communication among members of different cultures becomes even more acute when those communicating are from "high-context" and "low-context" communication cultures. In his book *Beyond Culture,* Hall (1977) defines a high-context communication culture (such as Japan) as one in which "most of the information is either in the physical context or internalized in the person, while very little is in the coded, explicit, transmitted part of the message" (p. 92). A low-context communication culture, on the other hand, is one in which "the mass of the information is vested in the explicit code" (p. 92). American culture, according to this definition is more a low-context than a high-context communication culture. Individuals from low- and high-context communication cultures often have difficulty in relating when they meet to solve a common problem. This is because low-context individuals pay more attention to the message and less to the context, while high-context individuals pay attention to movements and environmental aspects not noticed by others. For example, American managers dealing with Japanese employees need to realize that the highly codified behavior of the Japanese culture carries a message in itself.

Ethnocentrism and stereotyping

Ethnocentrism and stereotyping are related to one's perception of other cultures. Ethnocentrism is measuring other cultures against the yardstick of one's own culture and its behavioral norms. This can result in giving pejorative labels to others' customs and behaviors instead of seeing them as merely "different." For example, a manager who takes his or her management system as the norm and measures other management systems by this norm is promulgating ethnocentrism. Stereotyping, the attributing of qualities or characteristics to a person on the basis of group membership, can lead to misunderstanding and prejudice. Both ethnocentrism and stereotyping prevent flexibility of thinking and impartial evaluation of problems.

Culture shock

Culture shock is the experience of alienation a newcomer to a culture may have in regard to the host nationals, the language, the food, and the customs. Culture shock can lead to a rejection of the host nationals and an attempt to interact as much as possible with members of one's own culture. As a result, the cultural barrier is never bridged, and the newcomer may feel alienated and long to return to his or her native country.

Adaptability to a new culture depends upon a variety of factors. These include the ability to overcome culture shock and to have positive attitudes toward the new culture; efforts not to be ethnocentric and not to stereotype; skill in intercultural situations; a willingness to learn the new language and interact with the host nationals; and the attempt not to be judgmental about different patterns of reasoning and behavior. Successful adaptation also requires a high tolerance for ambiguous situations and sensitivity in dealing with new situations and with the host nationals.

Language skills

Persons who attempt to learn even a few words of the language of the host country often fare better than those who insist that the host nationals speak "their" language. It is not only a sign of politeness to learn the language of the host country, but also a good introduction to the culture of that country and an aid to better understanding of its people and customs.

Nonverbal communication

Nonverbal communication can speak as loudly as verbal communication. In fact, it can leave the wrong impression with host nationals, even if the verbal message does not. For example, a gesture that is acceptable in one culture may not be in another. Manners of listening and interacting may be different from culture to culture. Thus, managers need to recognize what is construed as obscene or offensive in various cultures and consciously avoid giving offense.

Interacting with host nationals

A willingness to interact with host nationals both on the job and during leisure hours facilitates adjustment to the new culture. Through this interaction valuable insight into the customs of the host nationals can be gained, thus saving the foreigner from making potentially embarrassing mistakes.

Differences in thinking and reasoning

Differences in thought patterns or forms of reasoning exist among cultures. The Aristotelian mode of reasoning is prevalent in the West but not in the East. Every culture may segment experience and approach problem-solving in a different fashion. For instance, a Japanese manager may think very differently from his or her American counterpart, so that what is construed as logical in one society may be perceived as illogical in another.

Different cultures also treat time and space differently. Some cultures are monochronic, while others are polychronic. Hall (1977) points out that monochronic cultures emphasize schedules, segmentation, and promptness. Time is treated as progressing in a linear fashion. Polychronic time cultures, in contrast, are characterized by several things happening at once. They stress involvement of people and transactions rather than adherence to preset schedules. American and northern European cultures are generally monochronic, while Arab, Turkish, and Latin American cultures tend to be polychronic. Managers who are accustomed to linear time progressions and strict schedules may feel frustrated in societies that place less value on time schedules.

Each culture also has an acceptable "space bubble" around its members. It is critical to know the proxemics (treatment of space) of a culture so that mistakes can be avoided. For example, Americans tend not to have a very close physical proximity to others during a conversation, especially if the business is not very personal. Close physical proximity is generally reserved for intimate conversation between husband and wife. However, such close physical proximity may be the norm in Latin America or the Middle East, and keeping one's distance can be perceived as insulting.

Cross-Cultural Transfer of Appropriate Technology

Cross-cultural problems regarding technology, particularly the transfer of technology, are unfortunately fairly common. Since this is such an important topic for students in engineering and business, we will consider it in some detail.

Engineers and managers are agents of change when they introduce new technology into a particular society or culture. This new technology has an impact upon the society or culture which receives it; that impact may be either positive or negative. As a result, those who provide technology to developing countries need to consider not just the kinds of technology they can provide, but the effects it will have on the recipient nations.

Donald Evans (1979) in his article, "Appropriate Technology and Its Role in Development," points out that "for the most part, imported, as opposed to domestic technology, is viewed as being more efficient and reliable" (p. 27). The reasons for this are (1) the imported technology must meet world standards to be competitive; (2) it is a proven technology that has withstood applications successfully in a variety of situations; (3) it is accompanied by management services and information essential to the developing country user; (4) maintenance, including replacements for consumable supplies, is provided by the supplier; and (5) depending upon the conditions of the technology transfer, the purchaser may be assured of continuing access to technological advances in the acquired product.

However, with the use of conventional foreign or imported technology, there may be two types of problems. One, Evans (1979) notes, may result from "the introduction of contemporary technology *per se*, and the other is associated with the choice of technology" (pp. 28-29). The first one maintains and even emphasizes the social and economic strata of a society; those citizens employed in foreign technology-based industry remain in a higher income stratum and have more political power than their rural counterparts. Technologies which are based in urban enclaves also contribute to inward migration to the cities from rural areas, with the resulting problems of overcrowding, substandard housing, increases in crime, and loss of family cohesion. Use of foreign technology may cause dependency on such a source, with a failure to train and provide for a local infrastructure of skilled employees to handle the technology.

The nonjudicious introduction of foreign technology can negatively affect a country's natural resource base and environment, just as the widespread use of dangerous pesticides can result in pollution of streams and lakes. Moreover, government policy, in its efforts to attract foreign technology (through protective tariffs or land grants) may distort the economy so that importation of foreign technology may be accomplished at the expense of one sector such as agriculture.

According to Evans (1979), the second problem, the choice of technology, is a critical one. Many times foreign technology is overscaled for the domestic market economy, resulting in inefficient use of invested capital that might have created more jobs. The products generated by the foreign technology may not be well suited for the domestic markets of developing countries, or they may not be affordable by the general population. On the other hand, products such as dishwashers and tape recorders may find a viable market but may be of questionable economic or social utility.

Overall, then, when a cross-cultural transfer of technology is to be made, managers must consider the following categories of potential problems: 1. an accelerated rate of depletion of the earth's natural resources; 2. threats to the environment; 3. problems of large-scale urbanization trends; 4. inappropriate allocation of capital; and 5. the alienation of humans from their natural habitat.

In contrast, the development of an appropriate technology must take place in a humanistic/conservator context. E. F. Schumacher, the founder of Intermediate Technology Development Group, states that "the most appropriate technologies in the prevailing circumstances of developing countries are more often likely to be a range of intermediate technologies which are more productive than the often highly labor-intensive but inefficient traditional technologies on the one hand but, on the other, are less costly and more manageable than the large-scale, labor-saving, and capital-intensive technologies of highly industrialized societies; and to be fully effective, these technologies will respond to local needs and factor endowments. In general, they will be cheaper and smaller, giving a wider, more equitable distribution of capital investment; they will create employment, providing work opportunities in areas where people live; they will foster the use of local capital, skills, and raw materials and reduce reliance on the importation of these factors; they will produce goods primarily for local consumption and use" (quoted in Evans 1979: 42–43).

W. H. Schacht, another expert, believes that "a balanced approach to appropriate technology requires that all types of technologies—advanced, intermediate, and basic—be considered in the promotion and policies of development. The choice of technology should be based not only on technological considerations and sophistication, but also on economic, cultural, environmental, energy, and social standards" (quoted in Evans 1979: 43). For example, developing nations have a labor force that is largely unemployed, underemployed, or unskilled; few capital assets (except for the OPEC countries); and a limited technological infrastructure to sustain technological growth. In addition, poor income distribution, small domestic markets, and a lack of marketing networks characterize the economics of developing countries. In contrast, the capital-intensive technologies of the industrialized countries are labor-saving and designed to promote efficiencies of scale. Therefore, for technology to be successful, it must involve those who will use it, and it must be custom tailored to fit the circumstances of the locale where it is to be applied.

INTEGRATION OF A CROSS-CULTURAL COMPONENT

How a cross-cultural component can be integrated in the curricula of engineering and business students depends upon the academic structure of the college or university in question. Offering an interdisciplinary course in intercultural relations, team-taught by instructors from the schools of business and engineering and the English department, is one method. The students would be both American and international students majoring in engineering and business (at the undergraduate and graduate levels). Academic credit would be given. The course could be proposed as an elective and, if successful, could become a required course.

Teaching intercultural skills: the instructors

Instructors for cross-cultural courses have had extensive contact with international students, and the instructor from the English department should be a specialist in English as a second language. These instructors should be given some cross-cultural training so that they are aware of the influence of culture on thinking and behavior. Margaret Pusch's article, "Cross-cultural training" (in *Learning Across Cultures*, edited by Gary Althen), is a valuable guide. Other resources include SIETAR (the Society for Intercultural Education, Training, and Research, 1414 22nd Street, N.W., Washington, D.C. 20037), a professional organization for individuals in intercultural education, training, and research. Films are available from a variety of sources, including the National Association for Foreign Student Affairs' "COMSEC Film List." Guest lecturers should be included whenever possible. These guests should be professionals in engineering and management who have had extensive work experience overseas.

Teaching and training methodologies

A variety of methodologies can be used for teaching cross-cultural issues, ranging from those highly structured by the teacher to those which are less structured and more participant oriented. Methods include the use of lectures, films, and videotapes, reading materials, structured experiences, outside assignments, brainstorming, group tasks, discussion groups, and case studies. Specific methods and topics will be discussed below.

Introduction to and discussion of skills required for effectiveness overseas. This would include all the skills mentioned earlier, and could be taught by a combination of lectures, films, and other audiovisual materials. Films that promote cultural awareness are very useful. Reading assignments should be about culture, intercultural communication, and specific topics of interest to the participants, such as transfer of technology.

Structured Experiences. A variety of structured experiences can be used. Whatever type is used must contain four basic steps to be successful. According to Margaret Pusch (in *Learning Across Cultures*, edited by Gary Althen), these four steps are (1) an introduction to the purposes and procedures of the experience; (2) the experience or action which then takes place; (3) an explanation by the participants of what they did during the experience as well as an expression of how they felt; and (4) a discussion in which participants interpret what happened and talk about why they responded as they did. The purpose of the last step is "to relate the experience to the issues that the experience was intended to illustrate, and to extract lessons that might be useful in other situations" (p. 88).

Role-playing is a good example of a structured experience. Role-playing involves a simple scenario in which participants play members of host and native countries. These "skits" usually last from five to ten minutes and often involve a "what if" exercise. Analysis follows the role-playing.

Critical incidents are another way to provide structured experiences. These are brief vignettes portraying situations of cultural conflict or misunderstandings. By focusing on real life issues, they involve the participants in problem-solving and discussion. For intance, these scenarios could center upon differences between high-context and low-context cultures or monochronic versus polychronic ones. Here are some examples:

Situation: Mr. Y, an American manager, is very pleased with the performance of Mr. Z, a Japanese employee, in his multinational company. Mr. Y praises Mr. Z in front of the other Japanese employees. Mr. Z is embarrassed rather than pleased. Why? What should Mr. Y have known about the status of the group versus the individual in Japanese culture? What should he have known about high-context and low-context communication cultures?

Situation: Mr. X, the manager of a firm doing business in Kuwait, is invited as a guest to the home of an influential businessman. At the dinner table, Mr. X uses his left hand to pass food to other guests. The host feels Mr. X has been deliberately insulting to him and to his guests. Why? What should Mr. X have known about right-hand versus left-hand uses in Arab countries?

Situation: An American businessman has an appointment for 10:30 A.M. with a Latin American government official. When the U.S. businessman arrives at 10:25 A.M., he discovers that he will have to wait for an indefinite period of time. Finally, thirty minutes later, he is admitted to the office of the government official only to find that several other persons are already there in conversation with the official. The Americn businessman is annoyed for two reasons. First, he has been kept waiting for a length of time that in his culture is considered an insult. Second, he expected to conduct his business in private with the government official. Instead, he found that he was expected to discuss private matters in front of several persons who were not connected to his business.

What should the American businessman have known about monochronic and polychronic cultures? What should he have known about proxemics in Latin American countries?

Outside assignments. These should focus upon either observing or interacting with members of the host culture. They can include observing people conversing, going to a store to purchase a needed item, or interviewing an official.

Brainstorming. Participants are asked to give immediate reactions to a problem or question. Then, when everyone has responded, the ideas can be discussed and evaluated, and appropriate choices can be made.

Discussion Groups. Usually, discussion groups are given a specific topic to consider. Topics can involve problem-solving situations such as those managers are likely to encounter in multinational companies. Other possible topics include stereotypes or value hierarchies, in which individual participants are asked to put random lists of items into a preferred order. For example, "The most important professions in my country are _____ ."

Case studies. The case study approach works very well in many business courses and some engineering courses, particularly those concerned with management theories and practices. Each student in the class is given the same case to study; one student is responsible for leading a class discussion about the case, summarizing, and analyzing it. The examples which follow are based on transfer of appropriate technology. Discussion can focus on whether or not the choice of technology was appropriate, whether or not the technology succeeded, and, if it did, what the reasons were for its success. The effects of the technology upon the locale and population should also be considered in the discussion. Participants should be encouraged to discuss several alternative solutions, more than one of which may be valid.

HAITI: THE COFFEE ROADS
(adapted from Adler 1979)

Haiti's economy is basically agricultural, and coffee is its most important commodity. The production and subsequent exportation of coffee provide close to $20 million in foreign exchange annually. Some regions with potential for coffee production were at one time inaccessible due to a lack of roads and subsequent market opportunities.

The construction of 110 kilometers of new penetration roads has facilitated the production of coffee in previously barren mountain areas in Haiti. The roads were built entirely by hand; no mechanized equipment was utilized on the project. The project used indigenous labor and materials and contained a training component which ensured that technicians capable of designing additional projects would remain in Haiti.

According to Chuck Pettis, chief engineer for the coffee roads project, there were several reasons to support the use of manual road building for this project: (1) funding was such that capital intensity, or even a mixture of capital and labor intensity, was prohibitive; (2) there was an abundance of underemployed workers in Haiti; (3) a high skill level was not required to hand-build roads if engineering and supervisory skills were present; (4) some of the mountain areas could not have been reached by machinery at the onset of the project; and (5) the intensive use of labor often creates a community spirit if villagers actually are involved in a development project and can feel responsible for the creation of a product.

In regard to the social and economic impact of the roads, the following positive effects were observed: prior to working on the coffee roads, most of the workers were subsistence farmers; many had never even received wages. The roads created both primary (road-building) and secondary (coffee farming) employment opportunities for nearly fifty villages. This resulted in villagers being better clothed and fed and being able to purchase their own land and buy cows and chickens. Schools, churches, and new homes have appeared in villages since temporary roads have brought vehicles into communities. Women, who were the traditional means of transportation of goods to market, are now free to perform other duties. It appears that a low middle class is being created in Haiti. In addition, the introduction of coffee centers has improved the soil conditions as previous deforestation had caused severe erosion. Finally, new roads have lowered the cost of transporting fertilizers.

On the other hand, some negative effects were also observed: land prices have increased substantially, and people who were satisfied with simple things now want more. Often, these increased desires lead to frustration and resulting high crime rates.

JAVA, INDONESIA: THE INTRODUCTION OF
RICE PROCESSING TECHNOLOGY
(adapted from Cain 1979)

Mechanized rice hullers were introduced in Java in order to modernize agriculture on the island and thus increase rice production. An adverse effect was that the introduction of this technology also created labor displacement, particularly among women who traditionally were involved in rice harvesting.

Although 60 percent of the total calories and 65 percent of the protein in the Indonesian diet comes from rice, domestic consumption of rice is higher than the country's capacity to produce it. Thus, rice must be imported to meet local demand. Most of the rice production is done with traditional, nonmechanical methods. But the mechanization of rice production in the tropics has many problems that still remain unsolved. Amir Khan of the International Rice Research Institute notes that "Attempts to transfer the highly advanced Western and Japanese mechanization technologies have not produced effective results for the small farm holdings in the tropical regions. The overwhelming need today is to develop an intermediate mechanization technology to suit the prevailing set of agricultural, socioeconomic, and industrial conditions of the tropical regions" (quoted in Cain 1979: 169).

USAID/Jakarta and the Indonesian government considered four efficient alternatives in order to modernize the rice marketing sector. The most capital-intensive required $65,000 investment per worker and the most labor-intensive required only $700 per worker. Many Western and Western-trained technicians identified capital-intensive with modern, and modern with good. (These value judgments may play an important role in determining technological choice.) The Indonesian government chose the mechanical but less high-technology alternative because it was economically preferable.

The initial cost of a huller in Pasawahan village in 1976 was about $4,000 U.S., and operating costs were low. At this hulling center or mill, about two tons of rice could be hulled per day—compared to the hand-pounding of forty kilograms per day by one woman. The average cost of hand pounding was $1.45 per 100 kilograms, while the average cost to the farmer of using a huller was $.54 per kilogram. The by-products were kept by the miller, while in the traditional harvest, women kept these by-products to use as animal feed.

In the five years of its operation, the mill had taken over work traditionally done by women of landless families from that village and neighboring ones. Estimates of jobs lost ranged as high as 1.2 million in Java alone and as high as 7.7 million in all of Indonesia. Loss to laborers in earnings due to use of hullers was $50 million annually in Java, representing 125 million woman-days of labor.

Although the rice farmer pays less to the mill for threshing and the process is much quicker, the problems of unemployment have been exacerbated. Women have lost an important source of income, and they are now forced to work longer hours at other jobs, if they can find them. The shift from a traditional technology to a more modern one has eliminated an important source of income for landless villagers.

Comparisons of these two case studies reveal important assumptions about technology and transfer of appropriate technology. In the example of road-building in Haiti, modern technology was adapted to fit the needs of the society, and it enhanced the living conditions of the villagers by providing job opportunities (both primary and secondary). In contrast, the introduction of a modern technology, mechanized rice hullers, has had a negative impact on Javanese society as a whole. Although a few have benefited from the lower cost and efficiency, the new technology has displaced a traditional female work force and has provided no alternative sources of income for them. What questions should have been asked by the managers in charge of this project before a decision about appropriate technology was made? What groups of village people should have been asked? How could the displacement of female workers have been prevented?

REFERENCES

Books on engineering, management, and intercultural studies

Althen, Gary (ed.), 1981. *Learning Across Cultures.* Washington: National Association for Foreign Student Affairs.

Brislin, Richard W. (ed.), 1977. *Culture Learning: Concepts, Applications, and Research.* Honolulu, HI: University Press of Hawaii.

Brislin, Richard W., and Paul Pedersen, 1976. *Cross-Cultural Orientation Programs.* New York: Gardner Press.

Burke, John G., and Marshall C. Eakin (eds.), 1979. *Technology and Change: Reader/Study Guide.* San Francisco, CA: Boyd & Fraser Publishing Co., Project of University Extension, University of California, San Diego.

Condon, J. C., and F. Yousef, 1975. *An Introduction to Intercultural Communication.* Indianapolis, IN: The Bobbs Merrill Co.

Cross-Cultural Communication: Implications for Language and Ethnic Studies, 1975. Report of a conference sponsored by the University of Massachusetts at Amherst with support of National Association for Foreign Student Affairs and Society for Intercultural Education, Training and Research.

Davenport, W. H., and D. Rosenthal (eds.), 1966. *Engineering: Its Role and Function in Human Society.* Department of Engineering, Reports Group, University of California, Los Angeles.

Goodman, Louis J., and Ralph N. Love (eds.), 1980. *Project Planning and Management.* New York: Pergamon Press, Pergamon Policy Studies on Socio-Economic Development.

Hall, Edward T., 1977. *Beyond Culture.* Garden City, NY: Anchor Books.

———, 1969. *The Hidden Dimension.* New York: Anchor Books.

———, 1959. *The Silent Language.* Greenwich, CT: Fawcett Books.

Harris, Philip R., and Robert T. Moran, 1979. *Managing Cultural Differences.* Houston: Gulf Publishing Co.

Hitti, P. K., 1971. *Islam: A Way of Life.* South Bend, IN: Gateway Editions, Ltd.

Hoopes, D. S. (ed.), 1971–1973. *Readings in Intercultural Communication,* Vol. I-III. Pittsburgh, PA: Regional Council for International Education, University of Pittsburgh.

Hsu, F. L. K., 1972. *American and Chinese*. La Jolla, CA: National History Publications Co.

Johnson, Dixon C., 1973–1974. "Ourselves and Others: Comparative Stereotypes." *International Educational and Cultural Exchange*, IX, 2–3 (Fall–Winter).

Landis, Dan, and Richard W. Brislin (eds.), 1983. *Handbook of Intercultural Training*, 2 vol. New York: Pergamon Press.

Miller, J. Dale, et al., 1979. *USA–Hispanic South America: Culture Capsules*. Rowley, MA: Newbury House Publishers, Inc.

Ruben, B. D., and R. W. Budd, 1975. *Human Communication Handbook: Simulations and Games*. Rochelle Park, NY: Hayden Book Co.

Trifonovitch, G., 1973. "On Cross-Cultural Orientation Techniques." *Topics in Culture Learning*, 225: 303–318.

Walsh, John E., 1979. *Humanistic Culture Learning: An Introduction*. Honolulu: University Press of Hawaii.

Articles and reports on management and intercultural studies

Almaney, Adan, 1974. "Intercultural Communication and the MNC Executive." *Columbia Journal of World Business* (Winter).

Alpander, F., 1973. "Drift to Authoritarianism: The Changing Managerial Styles of the U.S. Executive Overseas." *Journal of International Business Studies* (Fall).

Baker, J. C., and J. M. Ivancevich, 1970. "Multinational Management Staffing with American Expatriates." *Economic and Business Bulletin* (Fall).

——, 1971. "The Assignment of American Executives Abroad: Systematic, Haphazard or Chaotic?" California Management Review, XIII, 3: 39–44.

Beeth, G., 1973. "How to Build an Excellent International Staff." *International Management Practice*, AMACOM, 66–81.

David, K., 1972. "Effect of Intercultural Contact and International Stance in Attitude Change toward Host Nationals." *International Journal of Psychology*.

de Bettignies, H. C., and D. B. Louis, 1975. "Men at the Crossroads: Europe's Perspective." In Chapter 1 of *Management Development and Training Handbook*, edited by Taylor & Lippi. New York: McGraw-Hill.

Drucker, P. A., 1973. "What We Can Learn From Japanese Management." *The McKinsey Quarterly* (Winter).

Eldin, H. K., and S. Sadig, 1971. "Suggested Criteria for Selecting Management Consultants in Developing Countries." *International Management Review*, 4-5: 123–132.

Graves, D., 1972. "Cultural Determinism and Management Behavior." *Organizational Dynamics* (Autumn).

Harris, P. R., and D. L. Harris, 1976. "Intercultural Education for Multinational Managers." *International and Intercultural Communication Annual*. Speech Communication Association, 3 (Dec.): 70–85.

Hays, R. D., 1971. "Ascribed Behavioral Determinants of Success-Failure Among U.S. Expatriate Managers." *Journal of International Business Studies*, 2, 1 (Spring): 40–46.

Hildebrandt, H. W., 1973. "Communication Barriers Between German Subsidiaries and Parent American Companies." *Michigan Business Review* (July).

Howard, C. G., 1974. "Model for the Design of a Selection Program for Multinational Executives." *Public Personnel Management*, March-April: 138–145.

"How Firms Prepare Executives for Foreign Posts," 1970. *Business International*, Aug. 14: 262.

Ivancevich, J. M., and J. C. Baker, 1970. "A Comparative Study of the Satisfaction of Domestic United States Managers and Overseas United States Managers." *Academy of Management Journal*, March: 69–77.

Johnson, M. B., and G. L. Carter, Jr., 1972. "Training Needs of Americans Working Abroad." *Social Change* 2, 1: 1–3.

Renwick, G. W., 1976. "Australian and American Cultures: Similarities, Differences, Difficulties." *Intercultural Management Series*, No. 1: Intercultural Network, Inc., Scottsdale, AZ.

Simonetti, S. H., and J. Weitz, 1972. "Job Satisfaction: Some Cross-Cultural Effects." *Personnel Psychology*, 25: 107–118.

Stessin, Lawrence, 1973. "Culture Shock and the American Businessman Overseas." *International Educational and Cultural Exchange*, 1, 1 (Summer): 23–35.

Stoner, J. A., J. D. Aram, and I. M. Rubin, 1972. "Factors Associated with Effective Performance in Overseas Work Assignments." *Personnel Psychology*, 225: 303–318.

Vicker, R., 1973. "Understanding the Arab Psyche." *Wall Street Journal*, Oct. 19.

Wilce, H., 1971. "How to Ease the Culture Shock." *International Management*, June: 18–22.

Wsigand, R. T., and G. A. Barnett, 1976. "Multidimensional Scaling of Cultural Processes: The Case of Mexico, South Africa, and the United States. In *International and Intercultural Communication Annual*, edited by Fred L. Casmir. Vol. III, Falls Church, VA: Speech Communication Association: 139–172.

Zeira, Y., 1975. "Overlooked Personnel Problems of Multinational Corporations." *Colombia Journal of World Business*, Summer: 96–103.

Articles, books, and reports on transfer of appropriate technology

Adler, Laurie Nogg, 1979. "Haiti: The Coffee Roads." In Evans and Adler 1979: 129–150.

Alonso, Marcelo, 1978. "Technological Development: Concepts and Actions." *Approtech: Journal of the Association for the Advancement of Appropriate Technology for Developing Countries*, 1, 1 (Nov.): 3–6.

Asian Development Bank, 1977. "Appropriate Technology and its Application in the Activities of the Asian Development Bank."

Breach, Ian, 1977. "Technology and the Third World: Supplying the Right Kind of Aid." *The Financial Times* (London), 14 April: 25.

Cain, Melinda L., 1979. "Java, Indonesia: The Introduction of Rice Processing Technology." In Evans and Adler 1979:167–179.

Darling, H. S., 1975. "Appropriate Technology and Third World Agriculture." *Span*, 18, 3: 119–121.

Dickson, David, 1975. *The Politics of Alternative Technology*. New York: Universe Books.

Eckaus, Richard S., 1977. *Appropriate Technologies for Developing Countries*. Washington, D.C.: National Academy of Sciences.

Evans, Donald D., and Laurie Nogg Adler (eds.), 1979. *Appropriate Technology for Development: A Discussion and Case Histories*. Boulder, CO: Westview Press.

French, David, 1977. *Appropriate Technology in Social Context: An Annotated Bibliography*. Mt. Ranier, MD: VITA.

Fuglesang, Andreas, 1977. *Doing Things . . . Together: Report on an Experience in Communicating Appropriate Technology*. Uppsala: Dag Hammarskjold Foundation.

Jedlicka, Allen D., 1977. *Organization for Rural Development: Risk Taking and Appropriate Technology*. New York: Praeger.

Khan, Amir U., 1974. "Appropriate Technologies: Do We Transfer, Adapt or Develop?" In *Employment in Developing Nations: Report on a Ford Foundation Study*, edited by Edgar O. Edwards. New York: Columbia University Press, 223–233.

Love, Sam, 1974. "We Must Make Things Smaller and Simpler: An Interview with E. F. Schumacher." *Futurist*, 8, 6 (Dec.): 281–284.

McRobie, George, 1974. "Technology for Development—'Small is Beautiful.' " *Journal of the Royal Society of Arts*, 122 (March): 214–224.

Morss, Elliott R., et al., 1976. *Strategies for Small Farmer Development: An Empirical Study of Rural Development Projects in The Gambia, Ghana, Kenya, Lesotho, Nigeria, Bolivia, Colombia, Mexico, Paraguay and Peru*, vol. I. Boulder, CO: Westview Press.

O'Kelley, Elizabeth. "Appropriate Technology for Women of the Developing Countries." *Peace Corps Program and Training Journal*, 4, 6: 10–13.

_____, 1976. "Intermediate Technology as an Agent of Change: Simple Technologies, High Employment." In *Proceedings: The World Food Conference*, 505–513.

Rosenblatt, Samuel M. (ed.), 1979. *Technology and Economic Development: Realistic Perspective*. Boulder, CO: Westview Press.

Schlie, Theodore W., 1974. "Appropriate Technology: Some Concepts, Some Ideas, and Some Recent Experiences in Africa." *Eastern Africa Journal of Rural Development*, 7, 1–2, 77–108.

Schumacher, E. F., 1973. *Small is Beautiful: A Study of Economics as if People Mattered*. London: Blond and Briggs.

Steffens, J., 1976. "Development and Technology Transfer." New York: American Society of Mechanical Engineers, Paper No. 76-WA/TS-15.

United Nations Department of Economic and Social Affairs, 1974. *The Impact of Multinational Corporations on Development and on International Relations*. New York: United Nations.

Total Immersion of Welcome Outsiders: Cross-Cultural Encounters

David W. Gurney

Total immersion and cross-cultural encounters. How are these concepts viewed by the participants in an educational setting: the outsider and the teacher? What implications do differing perceptions have for teacher training for cross-cultural instruction, i.e., teaching English to speakers of other languages? A perspective may be gained from an orientation described by the American Association of Colleges of Teacher Education: at whatever level of instruction/learning, students' learning reflects, in large measure, what they bring into class with them from unique perspectives formed within a diversity of socioeconomic and cultural backgrounds. Education, then, has the potential for viewing, accepting (welcoming), and valuing students' unique perspectives on their own education, the school/college, and the society as a whole.

A rationale for teacher attitudes and training follows from this conceptualization: schools and educators should allow for maximum interaction between educational goals, content, techniques and personalities, and the cultural milieux which students represent. In essence, education must build on what the learner brings into the classroom in order to create optimum learning conditions for successful achievement.

Although there should be little argument about the above statement, teacher training for such cross-cultural interactions can take rather directed forms, such as specific training on one set of cultural variables (as if they will apply to every student from the culture who is enrolled in one's classes). Some methods are more like cookbook approaches, with specific selections, vignettes, or cultural events which show how people will get into trouble if they have not learned the proper response(s). Even training for nonverbal communication needs verbal back-up to develop nonverbal symbols as part of a total human communicative experience. So, too, teachers involved in cross-cultural communication or general education need a broader, less prescriptive, form of training.

Suggested here is an approach which builds equally on what the teacher brings to the teaching/learning cross-cultural encounter. The teacher should have a basic empathy for differences among cultures as well as a broad awareness of the American culture. Recent research on total immersion of Japanese high school students in the United States indicates that this basic empathy for cultures is as important a competence for members of the U.S. host community as a basic awareness of Japanese culture. Teachers and students agree that the third most important quality for cross-cultural teachers is a broad awareness of American culture.

Accepting students as "welcome outsiders" promotes the highest goals of education in this society by encouraging students to maintain a healthy cultural pride as well as by using interactions with these students to strengthen the validity of our differences and our similarities as human beings. Accepting students as equals in the teaching/learning process involves using their experiences to help them achieve meaningful social interactions. This approach does not require educators to have pre-conceived generalities about the students' culture(s) in order to make meaningful connections with language or cultural patterns.

Rather, it requires educators to spend time learning about various cultures directly from students in the classroom. If American teachers represent the culture of the United States well, there can be little danger of their making false assumptions about other cultural behaviors. It will be up to the students to piece together the puzzle of the new behavior and culture (C2) rather than the instructors puzzling over how to make something fit into their ill-formed notions about the students' cultures.

In short, we suggest an alternative approach to teacher training, one that concentrates on training for basic cultural empathy and on learning how to explore students' experiences for logical, cultural connections to the meaning of new language structures and vocabulary. Such training would include attention to socioeconomic and cultural patterns which may influence students' attitudes and achievements in the new cultural environment. Some factors to consider include:

- density and types of housing (and their quality)
- general standards of living
- occupations and income of parents
- educational background of parents
- cultural, ethnic, or ancestral background
- language(s) spoken at home
- family patterns and relationships
- family responsibilities of children
- leisure activities of family
- community attitudes, values, problems, unique features

Related to these factors, a comprehensive list of cultural events can be prepared in order to provide a basis for exposure to the new culture which the foreign students will constantly encounter during their period of total immersion. Such events as social occasions, work and daily living activities, special occasions, and a whole range of other patterns of life common to the English-speaking society in which the foreign student resides, can be explored for the purpose of setting up relevant experiences for the ESOL learner.

The approach we recommend would include a variety of competencies teachers might develop in order to provide sound learning environments in which foreign students can adjust to total English immersion. Competency in ethnography would help show how language is used for daily living and, thus, give insights on cultural patterns themselves. The students would be engaged in analysis and conceptualization about language and culture rather than just memorizing language patterns which fit simulated events. However, care should be taken to avoid the assumption that cultural elements analyzed through ethnographic techniques reflect a whole society or whole societal norm. Analysis and conceptualization should take a problem-posing form in order to involve ESOL students directly in their own reactions to new cultural experiences. Since total immersion creates a potent cultural matrix of student and teacher, teachers must learn how to deal with complex interactions from a conceptual as well as an empathetic point of view. The ability to conceptualize social patterns in order to help newcomers adjust as they learn the language which describes the patterns can be enhanced by the teacher's awareness of social and cultural change in the immediate community as well as the English-speaking society at large.

Beyond conceptualization of cultural patterns is the ability of the teacher to create cultural conditions for learning within contexts of meaningful language use. Any language used in classroom situations should focus on expressing the students' actual experiences (past, present, or future) rather than simply manipulating new language patterns to assess accuracy. In the final analysis, teaching grammar should be based on the idea of creating a cultural, not a linguistic, experience for the students. Teach grammar as culture, not as content.

The benefits to the suggested approach can be summarized as follows: teachers and learners would share together in the learning process, learning about each other, facilitating each other's tasks, and sharing in mutual successes. Control would fluctuate between teacher and students as needed.

Suggestions for specific training will be described below. They are based on an analysis of the difficulties experienced by foreign high school students who go through the conditions of total English immersion in the United States. Adjustment to daily use of English is seen within a broader range of experiences than just linguistic or functional communciation. There are, for example, the sociolinguistic dimensions of various domains and role relationships which influence the immersion encounters, and the climate for requesting and receiving help from members of the dominant society. ESOL students may not recognize that members of the new speech community use a variety of expressions, colloquialisms, and even totally different manners of speaking depending upon the level of formality, the purpose of the communicative act, and the participants—although they are probably aware of this phenomenon in their own cultures and countries.

Given this added barrier, the new speakers ("outsiders") may not overcome sometimes simple problems due to a lack of understanding when help is offered. Indeed, they may not seek help at all, or may ask for help from a less-qualified source about a problem in a different situation. For instance, students may ask help from other students about language problems with teachers. This may reflect more than a cultural hesitancy to question teachers. When one is trying to communicate, attention diverted to language form and vocabulary can compound an already hesitant initiative to speak.

Perhaps greater competence can be developed as learners are allowed to experiment with their incipient abilities, exploring a wide range of domains of language use and relationships with native speakers of the new language. Mistakes will occur during such exploration. But it is within the context of mistakes, social as well as linguistic, that a person learning a new behavior often discovers and internalizes the proper modes of behavior. If tolerance for mistakes is not evident, and help is directed primarily at language form instead of helping the student to remove barriers to communication, difficulties may increase. Indeed, some foreign students may have less than average motivation to share in the social life of their new surroundings.

Rather than consisting of a haphazard race through a sociolinguistic, grammatical, and lexical minefield, immersion conditions could involve native models in planned interaction with foreign students, and facilitation of cross-cultural integration by focusing on sharing cultural and personal perspectives. Teachers could select concepts to serve as the basis for concentrated language practice, deriving language from life rather than extending language manipulation to "meaningful" communication episodes. In this way, language will evolve from meaningful, personal experiences.

Now, let us look at a few ways that the suggested approach might work in an ESOL classroom. Our goal is to integrate a variety of techniques: ethnography, establishing cultural context, problem-posing, and functional/daily living patterns. Underlying all of these is a constant focus on meaningfulness through the use of students' experiences in English learning.

Where does one start? Well, consider the learner who wants to become competent in English. Where does this person start? He or she has a smoothly working physiological system for producing language; however, in learning a new language, much of the physiological patterning will change. Not all of it has to change, because we human beings have much in common, even when our languages differ as much as Japanese differs from English. (The Japanese say, "The restaurant, where is it?" At first, this may sound strange. But in English, we frequently highlight our topic in a similar way: "The restaurant. Where is it again?") So, the learner starts with a full set of language-producing patterns, and millions of personal experiences—any of which can be triggered by an appropriate referent, image, symbol, etc. How do we stimulate and make use of these experiences?

Let us go back to ethnography and cultural conditions of common experiences. If our purpose is to teach the way in which reality is perceived, sequenced, or reacted to in this country, we can select a common event to demonstrate cultural reality—e.g., delivery of a newspaper. We could easily create a mock house, people inside, and an American in a mock car or bike throwing a newspaper on the driveway. Not very cultural, you say? Think about the language used when the paper goes into the bushes, a puddle, or a window!

Have the students note the time of day, who reads the paper, who takes it to work, etc. (You are teaching them to use ethnography-observation techniques within normal cultural conditions.) Next, indicate one of the students' native countries on a map. Ask a student from that country to enact a similar scene from his or her homeland. As the student acts, describe what is happening in English, focusing on relevant language forms, e.g., the verbal: he is coming up the street, he is throwing, I am reading, etc. Then have a few students from other countries share their cultural patterns.

Now you are ready to develop some language control. Note that many of the students will have already perceived what the pattern means. Using the scenarios everyone in class has witnessed, model a sentence which uses the desired language form, and describes one of the actions within a specific cultural context: "Here we are in Japan. The family is eating breakfast." Model the sentence two or three times, then have the students repeat it. Ask, "What is the family in Japan eating?" and elicit a response. Have the students ask and answer questions among themselves. When control of the model sentence is sufficient, change the country. Let students describe where the family is eating breakfast. (It's not hard to add a preposition and teach them to say, "The family is eating breakfast in China.") Continue changing the countries to include every student's homeland. At this point, control of the model should be complete.

The names of different countries could be used as test stimulants to see how well students have learned the pattern. However, further variations can also be added to extend the cultural context and provide more practice with the grammatical pattern. For example, show pictures or use re-enactments to provide a setting for variations of the pattern, such as: the man is driving along the street, or he is throwing the newspaper on the sidewalk. (Variations of location can be used to extend practice here. This is not an appropriate time to try to develop mastery of *I, he, she, we, they am/is/are* throwing.) The variations could number 4-6 and should all be repeated. Then use them for a simple substitution drill.

At this point, the students should have considerable control over the subject + aux + *-ing* pattern in English. Then attempt to verify their ability to use the pattern in meaningful communication. Ask students to describe actions. Do not simply ask, "What is the man throwing?", if you can see a newspaper in the stimulus picture. Model the answer using the name of a local paper. Then ask the question, indicating that you want the student to name a newspaper from his or her native country, such as "The man is throwing the *Daily Yomiuri* newspaper." Upon being shown a stick figure of a person reading a newspaper, a student could state, "Tsutomo (his uncle) is reading the *Daily Yomiuri* newspaper."

The newspaper provides a broad basis for developing global awareness (an alternative cross-cultural approach) as a purpose for communicative competence. Many comparisons and similarities between cultures can be exploited for cross-cultural understanding and meaningful language practice. Creative variations are only limited by the extent of teachers' own sociolinguistic, syntactic, and lexical competence. Teachers must become masters of the patterns and contexts of communication in order to focus student attention on meaning and not merely on grammatical, syntactic, or lexical symbols, paradigms, or rules. Language control, then, can be achieved through familiar and, gradually, new behavior patterns for daily life.

As we realize that each person's behavior is both unique and like our own; that communication is more than just linguistic, cultural, social or familial; and that each person is, in effect, a self-educated individual, we will find more ways to teach language through basic linguistic competence and personal and shared human responses. Each of us will be outsiders and, through tolerance, can become "welcome outsiders."

REFERENCES

Crawford-Lange, Linda M., 1981. "Redirecting Second Language Curricula: Paulo Freire's Contribution." *Foreign Language Annals,* 14, 4 & 5: 257–268.
Finocchiaro, Mary, and Michael Bonomo, 1973. *The Foreign Language Learner: A Guide for Teachers.* New York: Regents Publishing Company.
Gurney, David W., 1970. "Linguistic Adjustment and Language Background of American Field Service Students in the United States, 1969–70." *Dissertation Abstracts* 31 (9A), 4747.
_____, 1979. "Total Immersion of Foreign High School Students in the United States: Sociolinguistic Implications." *Linguistics* 17: 337–346.
_____, 1984. Linguistic Adjustment of YFU Japanese Students in the United States, 1983–84, Report of Research (unpublished).
Hendon, Ursula, 1980. "Introducing Culture in the High School Foreign Language Classroom." *Foreign Language Annals,* 13, 3: 191–199.
Hickey, Leo, 1980. "Ethnography for Language Learners." *Foreign Language Annals,* 13, 6: 475–481.
Hunter, William A. (ed.), 1974. *Multicultural Education Through Competency-based Teacher Education.* Washington, D.C.: American Association of Colleges for Teacher Education.
Hymes, Dell (ed.), 1964. *Language in Culture and Society.* New York, NY: Harper and Row Publishers.
Jakobovits, Leon A., and Barbara Jordan, 1974. *The Context of Foreign Language Teaching.* Rowley, MA: Newbury House Publishers.
Joiner, Elizabeth Garner, and Patricia Barney Westphal (eds.), 1978. *Developing Communication Skills.* Rowley, MA: Newbury House Publishers.

Krashen, Stephen D., 1983. *Principles and Practice in Second Language Acquisition*. Elmsford, NY: Pergamon Press.

Oller, John W., Jr., and Jack C. Richards (eds.), 1973. *Focus on the Learner: Pragmatic Perspectives for the Language Teacher*. Rowley, MA: Newbury House Publishers.

Wallerstein, Nina, 1983. *The Teaching Approach of Paulo Freire*. In *Methods That Work*, edited by John W. Oller, Jr., and Patricia A. Richard-Amato. Rowley, MA: Newbury House Publishers, 190–204.

Wardhaugh, Ronald, 1976. *The Contexts of Language*. Rowley, MA: Newbury House Publishers.

NTC PROFESSIONAL MATERIALS

ACTFL Review

Published annually in conjunction with the American Council on the Teaching of Foreign Languages

NEW PERSPECTIVES, NEW DIRECTIONS IN FOREIGN LANGUAGE EDUCATION, ed. Birckbichler, Vol. 20 (1990)

MODERN TECHNOLOGY IN FOREIGN LANGUAGE EDUCATION: APPLICATIONS AND PROJECTS, ed. Smith, Vol. 19 (1989)

MODERN MEDIA IN FOREIGN LANGUAGE EDUCATION: THEORY AND IMPLEMENTATION, ed. Smith, Vol. 18 (1987)

DEFINING AND DEVELOPING PROFICIENCY: GUIDELINES, IMPLEMENTATIONS, AND CONCEPTS, ed. Byrnes, Vol. 17 (1986)

FOREIGN LANGUAGE PROFICIENCY IN THE CLASSROOM AND BEYOND, ed. James, Vol. 16 (1984)

TEACHING FOR PROFICIENCY, THE ORGANIZING PRINCIPLE, ed. Higgs, Vol. 15 (1983)

PRACTICAL APPLICATIONS OF RESEARCH IN FOREIGN LANGUAGE TEACHING, ed. James, Vol. 14 (1982)

CURRICULUM, COMPETENCE, AND THE FOREIGN LANGUAGE TEACHER, ed. Higgs, Vol. 13 (1981)

Professional Resources

CENTRAL STATES CONFERENCE TITLES (annuals)

A TESOL PROFESSIONAL ANTHOLOGY: CULTURE

A TESOL PROFESSIONAL ANTHOLOGY: GRAMMAR AND COMPOSITION

A TESOL PROFESSIONAL ANTHOLOGY: LISTENING, SPEAKING, AND READING

THE COMPLETE ESL/EFL RESOURCE BOOK, Scheraga

ABC'S OF LANGUAGES AND LINGUISTICS, Hayes, et al.

AWARD-WINNING FOREIGN LANGUAGE PROGRAMS: PRESCRIPTIONS FOR SUCCESS, Sims and Hammond

PUZZLES AND GAMES IN LANGUAGE TEACHING, Danesi

GUIDE TO SUCCESSFUL AFTER-SCHOOL ELEMENTARY FOREIGN LANGUAGE PROGRAMS, Lozano

COMPLETE GUIDE TO EXPLORATORY FOREIGN LANGUAGE PROGRAMS, Kennedy and DeLorenzo

INDIVIDUALIZED FOREIGN LANGUAGE INSTRUCTION, Grittner and LaLeike

LIVING IN LATIN AMERICA: A CASE STUDY IN CROSS-CULTURAL COMMUNICATION, Gorden

ORAL COMMUNICATION TESTING, Linder

ELEMENTARY FOREIGN LANGUAGE PROGRAMS: AN ADMINISTRATOR'S HANDBOOK, Lipton

PRACTICAL HANDBOOK TO ELEMENTARY FOREIGN LANGUAGE PROGRAMS, Second edition, Lipton

SPEAK WITH A PURPOSE! Urzua, et al.

TEACHING LANGUAGES IN COLLEGE, Rivers

TEACHING CULTURE: STRATEGIES FOR INTERCULTURAL COMMUNICATION, Seelye

TEACHING FRENCH: A PRACTICE GUIDE, Rivers

TEACHING GERMAN: A PRACTICAL GUIDE, Rivers, et al.

TEACHING SPANISH: A PRACTICAL GUIDE, Rivers, et al.

TRANSCRIPTION AND TRANSLITERATION, Wellisch

YES! YOU CAN LEARN A FOREIGN LANGUAGE, Goldin, et al.

LANGUAGES AT WORK (VIDEO), Mueller

CULTURAL LITERACY AND INTERACTIVE LANGUAGE INSTRUCTION (VIDEO), Mueller

For further information or a current catalog, write:
National Textbook Company
a division of *NTC Publishing Group*
4255 West Touhy Avenue
Lincolnwood, Illinois 60646-1975 U.S.A.